Endorsements

"Driven to succeed? *The Renegade Leader* will get you there. Today's leaders need adaptability to manage change. Jim Saunders' struggle to gain agreement from his team for a merger left me laughing and later applauding his success. While offering nine practical steps to influence people, ignite performance, and impact results, *The Renegade Leader* is a fun read as well!"
Barbara Trautlein, Ph.D., Principal, Change Catalysts LLC, Author of, *You Know Your IQ But What's Your CQ: Develop Change Intelligence to Catalyze Powerful Change in Your Career, Team, and Organization.*

"As a world class athlete and trainer of Olympian champions I know you can't win without a passion for excellence, a hunger for progress, and the ability to be confident, focused, and energized. *The Renegade Leader* will activate your inner flame for success and keep your eye on the gold."
Dr. JoAnn Dahlkoetter, Sports Psychologist, Best-selling Author of, *Your Performing Edge*

"If you want to compete with market leaders, grow your business, and succeed, you need the right mindset. *The Renegade Leader* gives today's leaders a window into the mindset shifts needed to be successful with today's workforce and to be respected for the leaders they are."
Don Staley, Best-Selling Author of, *Fit Mind, Fit Body*

"*The Renegade Leader* gives you the formula to move forward and get powerful results. Many leaders can come up with a great vision but are unsure how to get there. Just getting their people on board to join them on the journey can be difficult. *The Renegade Leader* helps you put your destination in sight, align your people to your vision, and make note of the mile-markers along the way. *The Renegade Leader* helped give me the confidence to move my people forward, fully on board, on a path that they had not expected. I heartily recommend that all business leaders read it."

Gina Hiatt, PhD
President, Finish Agent, Inc.

"Leadership expectations and best practices have evolved since I was a senior VP at General Electric Capital Corporation. Today's leaders are looking for ways to navigate new trends in leadership *and* live a fulfilling life while doing it. *The Renegade Leader* can free you from the confines of leadership and give you the opportunity to create better balance in your life."

Keiko Hsu, Founder and CEO
Wings for Women

"Renegade Leaders may be the type of catalyst that can get things off the status quo, find better solutions, and move more quickly. People will follow and believe in an exciting leader, especially if integrity and character are also a part of the equation. What a powerful combination that would be! Our current system is not working well, especially in corporate America. We have lost ground. I know I speak for myself and others I have worked with; people are ready for a return again to character and integrity. People I know have lost faith in our institutions. I believe people are starving for good leadership. In the organizations I have seen, so much is left on the table due to politics, ineffective leadership, and inability to execute. It is easier to be less accountable, less compassionate, and less moral. As a nation, we need to be looking at ourselves in the mirror. We can do and be better than we are. We have settled for less for quite a while, and it is showing in our economy and in our work climates. As for feedback about *The Renegade Leader*, I have been told I am a closet rebel, so it appealed to me on that level. I reacted to it immediately. I felt relief and hope. If you are a renegade, you are probably moving in the right direction. Pushing the envelope. Going for the extraordinary. Thank God. Someone is actually going to *do* something. Bring it on! And it can't be too soon!"

Jan Maunder, Executive

"Everyone will tell you that the key to creating sustainable transformations in your workplace is effective communication. The question is what type of communication? *The Renegade Leader* shows you how you can use transparent communication as a means to promote employee engagement to ignite high performance. A must-read for leaders of all types."

Skip Weisman, CEO
The leadership and workplace communication expert

"*The Renegade Leader* is as dynamic and energetic as its author. Debora put all of the secrets she uses to ignite people, performance, and profits into one book. The only thing missing

is the magic dust she provides that brings calm to chaos and creativity to confusion!"
Cyndi Fine
The BodyMind Connection

"Strategy is the heart of every organization; without it, you lack a roadmap to success. But even the best strategies can leave you lost without the alignment of your people. *The Renegade Leader* gives you the guidance you need to motivate your teams and to gain alignment so you can drive organizational results without driving yourself or your people crazy!"
Terry Schmidt, founder, StrategicPlanningAcademy.com
Author of *Strategic Project Management Tools Made Simple: Practice Tools for Leaders and Teams*

"Showing up as a Renegade Leader is part of being a courageous leader. Debora is a true renegade, who exudes dynamic appeal, from her black leather coat to the edgy sentences in *The Renegade Leader*. Different from other how-to leadership books, *The Renegade Leader* leads you on a journey through the inner world of its character, Jim Saunders, and pulls back the curtain on the day-to-day struggles of a CEO while offering engaging solutions. Debora sets the tone for a new breed of leadership, and *The Renegade Leader* draws a line in the sand—daring you to cross."
Laurie Cozart
Dynamic Appeal Communications

"Debora is doing the work that she was born for when she applies her personal, unique genius that enables leaders to excel. She has amazing gifts that guide leaders to change their communication and behavioral style so their message is heard, while building collaboration where chaos once existed around them. Get some of her personal genius for yourself when you read this book. *The Renegade Leader* will shift the human dynamics in your organization and help you become the leader others choose to follow. Cover to cover or one chapter at a time, you will be entertained, educated, and enlightened. Debora is brilliant, effective, and very fun—and so is her book."

Brenda Scarborough
The Thing You Were Born For, Helping You Live Your Life Purpose

"This book offers the perfect blend of Renegade Leadership while bringing the softer side of leadership. Creating awareness of emotional intelligence, appreciative inquiry, and neuroscience strategies, *The Renegade Leader* shows you how to shift from command to collaboration and competition to productivity. *The Renegade Leader* offers an artful approach to leadership, and its messages come alive in the story of Jim Saunders, who also softens around the edges and builds an organization that becomes a family. This book opens our eyes and hearts for a new way of leading that produces results and fulfillment for everyone involved. A must-read if you want success in your organization that looks and feels good."

Joy Perreras
Relaxing into Success mentor

"*The Renegade Leader* describes the leader who stands out from the crowd, whose courage and determination sets them apart from their competitors. Debora combines a contrarian voice with a sense of humor about the shifts needed in today's

leadership in order to create sustainable businesses and a better world. It makes for a great read and will leave a wake of I.N.F.L.U.E.N.C.E. behind."
Beth Banning CEO

"Leadership is an outer and inner game. *The Renegade Leader* addresses both how to become an inspired and innovative leader yourself while working the outside game of fostering leadership at all levels. Sometimes the biggest block can be yourself. *The Renegade Leader* shows you who you need to be to get the results you desire and hold up the mirror to your biggest potential."
Irena O'Brien, Ph.D.
Get Out of Your Own Way expert and business coach

"My clients tell me that they finally see their true and authentic selves for the first time through my lens. *The Renegade Leader* and Debora McLaughlin does just that, she lets leaders see themselves in a new light, gain a deeper perspective, and create a vision for themselves and for their organization that exceeds their initial expectations. *The Renegade Leader* puts the spotlight on leadership and offers it a new angle—one that can't be missed!"
Steve Cozart
The Camera-Ready Life: Inspired Business Portraits

"Leaders, teams, and organizations can maximize their results when united by common values and focus on the 'being' of leadership. *The Renegade Leader* offers a nine-step Framework that will refuel your passion for leadership and have you enjoy some laughs along the way. Who knew the power of presence could exist in a 200-page book and the giant shifts in leadership its five-foot, three-inch author is capable of making? A must-read for anyone willing to discover the true meaning of leadership."

Susan Hayward
CEO, Susan Hayward Now
Creator of The Protocol: Daily Strategies for Optimal Living

The Renegade Leader

Also coauthored by Debora J. McLaughlin

*Blueprint for Success: Proven Strategies
for Success & Survival*

Straight Talk for Getting Results

Roadmap for Career Success

Forthcoming Books:

Renegade Leaders Unleashed

No Winner Ever Got There Without a Coach
(coauthored with David Rock)

The Renegade Leader

9 SUCCESS STRATEGIES DRIVEN LEADERS USE
To Ignite People, Performance & Profits

Debora J. McLaughlin

BALBOA.
PRESS

A DIVISION OF HAY HOUSE

ISBN: 978-1-4525-5240-8 (sc)
ISBN: 978-1-4525-5241-5 (hc)
ISBN: 978-1-4525-5239-2 (e)

Library of Congress Control Number: 2012909252

Balboa Press books may be ordered through booksellers or by contacting:

Balboa Press
A Division of Hay House
1663 Liberty Drive
Bloomington, IN 47403
www.balboapress.com
1-(877) 407-4847

Because of the dynamic nature of the Internet, any web addresses or links contained in this book may have changed since publication and may no longer be valid. The views expressed in this work are solely those of the author and do not necessarily reflect the views of the publisher, and the publisher hereby disclaims any responsibility for them.

The author of this book does not dispense medical advice or prescribe the use of any technique as a form of treatment for physical, emotional, or medical problems without the advice of a physician, either directly or indirectly. The intent of the author is only to offer information of a general nature to help you in your quest for emotional and spiritual well-being. In the event you use any of the information in this book for yourself, which is your constitutional right, the author and the publisher assume no responsibility for your actions.

Any people depicted in stock imagery provided by Thinkstock are models, and such images are being used for illustrative purposes only. Certain stock imagery © Thinkstock.

Printed in the United States of America

Balboa Press rev. date: 7/17/2012

For my son, Alec McLaughlin, a true renegade who sees possibilities unseen by others, who navigates toward opportunities in the road less taken, and whose strength, courage, and likeability guarantee his success.

"Leadership is influence."

John C. Maxwell

Contents

Endorsements i

Foreword xix

Preface xxiii

Introduction 1

Chapter 1. Leadership: An Endless Exercise in Steering
Corrections 7

Chapter 2. Inspire Leadership: Creating the Spark 25

Chapter 3. Nourish Trust: Gaining Sure-Footed Traction in
Your Organization 39

Chapter 4. Foster Leadership at All Levels: Embracing the
Highest Standards 57

Chapter 5. Listen to Quiet or Unfamiliar Voices: Tuning into
the Hum of Your Engine 69

Chapter 6. Unleash the Potential in Your People: Shifting into
Overdrive 81

Chapter 7. Engage in Transparent Communication: Sharing the
Authentic Spirit of Navigation 95

Chapter 8. Notice and Recognize Achievements: Celebrating
the Mile Markers along the Way 109

Chapter 9. Create a Culture of Collaboration: Teaming up for
Championship Performance 119

Chapter 10. Enjoy and Respect Diversity: Developing Cultural
Intelligence 131

Chapter 11. Put it All Together: Living the
I.N.F.L.U.E.N.C.E. Framework 141

Epilogue 147

About the Author.. 159

Working with Debora... 163

Resources 165

Acknowledgments... 167

Index 171

Foreword

Dr. Bob Uslander
Founder and CEO, Doctors on Purpose

You absolutely deserve to be in the driver's seat of your life. As a leader today, you face a wealth of challenges. You are trying to do more with less; the daily pace is faster than ever; and the needs and demands of your employees, customers, and stakeholders can quickly take its toll. Whether you were promoted up the ranks of the organization you lead or are the CEO/owner of your own business, you've most likely discovered that leading others is more challenging than you expected. Not everyone is willing to follow your prescribed methods. Low employee engagement and lack of motivation can lead to a slow death for many organizations. *The Renegade Leader* is just what the doctor ordered to put the charge back into your organization and, along the way, deepen your own passion for being a great leader. In this brilliant book, Debora McLaughlin will help you discover your own inner capacity to lead and uncover the gifts you were meant to share as the leader of your organization and in your life.

It's never too late to create the life you are meant to be living—a life filled with purpose and passion. The key to having authentic success is learning to follow your inner guidance system as you navigate unexpected turns and maneuver around the obstacles that present themselves and seem determined to keep you from achieving your goals. *The Renegade Leader* gives you the added leverage you need, serving as your roadmap, sharing the shortcuts driven leaders use to ignite people, performance, and profits.

As an emergency physician for over 20 years and the founder and CEO of Doctors on Purpose, I coach physicians on how to create life balance, authentic happiness, and success, while finding meaning and joy in their careers and lives.

Most doctors went into medicine because they truly wanted to help people; they wanted to do what they love doing every day. But these days, so much about succeeding as a doctor seems the opposite of that. It's very stressful and very demanding, and many doctors have become overwhelmed and feel trapped.

It's easy for doctors to blame the "system" for their dissatisfaction; many feel like victims. That's how I felt for a number of years, until I had an epiphany. In one brilliant moment, I realized that I absolutely deserved to have a successful and abundant life. I finally understood that it was completely up to me to create that success and abundance. No one else was going to do it for me. I also understood that to achieve the success and abundance I wanted, I needed to learn new concepts, I needed to be willing to make changes and take risks, and I needed to surround myself with people who understood and lived by these same principles. Now, I challenge you to do the same. Be hungry to learn. Be open to change. Become the leader you were meant to be. Let *The Renegade Leader* show you the way.

The Renegade Leader introduces you to the I.N.F.L.U.E.N.C.E. Framework and offers the complete cure to most organizational challenges. Your organization is a collective group of systems; it has a living and breathing culture, a backbone of strategy, and a framework of technology that supports it. Sometimes, these systems can shift out of alignment. When this happens, just like a patient in the ER, the organization needs to arrive at a proper diagnosis and prescribe the appropriate treatment.

A renegade herself, Debora combines the passion and vision that allowed her to become a nationally recognized top sales performer. She understands how to drive business results. Her expertise in neuroscience and as a board-certified psychotherapist allows her to joyfully maximize employee engagement, promote behavior change, and reenergize the organizations she works with. She loves what she does and extends her reach through her Executive Coaching, Renegade Leader Roundtable Masterminds, and leadership development and business building groups.

Through her writing, Debora's energy, zest, and commitment to success jump off every page. Each chapter provides forward movement actions, making sure the information she provides leads to clear transformation. With a flair for engaging her readers, Debora shares how-to information within the entertaining tale of CEO Jim Saunders and his attempt to implement the I.N.F.L.U.E.N.C.E. Framework in his own organization. You might recognize yourself in his inner dialogue or laugh at his encounters with employees.

So, if you are a high achieving professional who appears to have it all, but you know that you and your organization haven't truly reached your potential, *The Renegade Leader* is for you. It will challenge you to push through to your personal best and unlock the true potential in you and your management team, while allowing you to create new levels of profitability and success. As a result, the pulse of your organization will rivet with possibility, creativity, and collaboration.

Remember how passionate you were when you first began your journey as a leader? Wouldn't you love to feel that passion again?

You can—when you lead on purpose and with intention. *The Renegade Leader* takes you on a path of self-awareness that will allow you to revitalize yourself and your organization. Discover the true leader within, and learn to see your organization in a new light. Transform yourself from being a victim of change to becoming a powerful master of change.

Lead with purpose. Lead with passion. Lead like a renegade. Begin today. Just turn the page and take the first step.

Preface

I can vividly remember standing on Wall Street at age 22, oversized buttered bagel in hand, the buildings crowding out the sunlight and towering high above my five-foot, three-inch frame. There I was, on my way to meet with an executive on the upper floors of a skyscraper, armed only with some product knowledge and sales training, wide shoulder pads, and oversized earrings.

I was a small town girl from upstate New York, and I was new to sales, new to my job at Digital Equipment Corporation (DEC), and new to the city. The client I was going to meet had recently thrown a sales rep out of his office, complaining that she must have "grown up on a farm." How would he react to me?

As a woman in the male-dominated information technology industry, I was already at a disadvantage. Most of my colleagues were men, and the leaders of the organizations I called on were men. It was an era when expense accounts were endless, and the people seated at three-martini business lunches in dark-paneled restaurants were also men. Without good survival skills, I knew that the competition (or the alcohol-laden lunches) would do me in.

Fortunately, I was a fast learner and had already figured out that success in sales in that town, in that era, against my competitors was going to take something more than the ability to memorize product information or list features and benefits.

So, unlike many of my competitors, who wined and dined at the top level, I built relationships up, down, and sideways in the organizations I served. Rather than focus on selling the fastest processor, I questioned the man in accounts payable on what motivated *him*—which was getting his work done faster so that he could get home in time for dinner. I made sure I cultivated relationships with not only the executives, technology managers, and department heads, but also the purchase order employee in the basement of the building. I sold products that satisfied personal needs instead of selling the latest technology.

As a result, I succeeded that fateful day in New York in creating a business partnership with the executive on that top floor, who sat at his giant desk surrounded by walls of glass that showcased the city. It was my first major sale.

Later, as I moved into Boston and into the high tech wave of telecommunications, this commitment to creating relationships landed me an $8 million sale, even though my supervisor at the time told me not to even try for it. That sale involved implementing voice, data, video, and training in 33 countries. It also required that I, as a National Account Manager, manage many others in order to make it happen.

The road wasn't always that smooth, though. When I became a leader, I had some hard lessons to learn. Like many leaders of high integrity, when something did not go well, I pushed, and my teams pushed back. It was a rude awakening to discover that the remote field engineers secretly referred to me as "the barracuda" because of my bulldog tenacity. I had little patience for error even when mishaps were expected. Suddenly, there I was facing the fact that I had become just a little bit like the client I had dreaded meeting that first day out in New York.

I had to relearn to treat my teams in the same manner I treated my customers, building relationships with them with the highest level of respect and with the same commitment to their success. I never made my clients feel "wrong"; why would

I rough up my own support teams? I learned to be patient and to ask for and listen to feedback on how we could implement schedules that were realistic and achievable. I learned to show appreciation for all of my team's efforts and to communicate openly about our mutual needs.

Now, for more than 25 years, I have used all of this experience, as well as my expertise in cognitive behavioral therapy (how to change thoughts, emotions, and behaviors for quick results) and study of neuroscience, to align people with their organizational vision, build the behaviors needed for success, and create cultures of collaboration and creativity. The Renegade Leaders I work with not only achieve their visions; they lead with greater influence and impact.

In his famous Stanford University commencement speech, Steve Jobs talked about connecting the dots of his life. It made me think of the "dots" in my own life. If I didn't know how to create sales, I wouldn't know how to get business results for my clients. If I hadn't studied psychology, I might not understand what motivates people or how to shift the thoughts, beliefs, and behaviors needed for high performance and increased employee engagement. If I hadn't led poorly in the past, I wouldn't have studied effective leadership and learned how to help others become the leader people choose to follow.

I don't have an MBA, and I didn't study at Harvard. What I know about leadership was learned in the trenches, not the classroom, and I've found this to be true of most of the Renegade Leaders I serve.

Over the years, I have seen the evolution of the demands on leaders, and from an objective, outside perspective, I have been able to provide the solutions that get leaders on the fast track to influencing people, igniting performance, and impacting profits.

It is my hope that *The Renegade Leader* will give you what you need to take on the challenges of leadership so that you can motivate those around you; deeply understand your employees, peers, and customers; position yourself as a top performer; and gain recognizable business results along the way. Email me at Debora@TheRenegadeLeader.com, and let me know what you have discovered about yourself on your leadership journey. Tell me what you tried, what worked, what didn't work, or simply join our conversation blog at www.TheRenegadeLeader.com to share your thoughts, challenges, and successes. I look forward to hearing your story.

Introduction

The day the title of this book, *The Renegade Leader*, was born, I was on the phone with a CEO I'd been coaching. I told him I was working on a new book and vividly described my vision of a Renegade Leader. He was quiet for a moment, and because he was rarely a man of few words, I wondered if I had offended him. Then, he exhaled and said, "You just described me to a 'T.'" Right then and there, I knew I was on to something.

Leaders today face unprecedented challenges. Economic downturns, changes in workforce demands, and an ever increasing competitive market—combined with the need to do more with less—make for trying times for the best of leaders. Those who stand out are the ones who take a stand and make a difference. I call these exceptional people "Renegade Leaders."

True Renegade Leaders drive results, instill trust within their organizations, allow innovative thinking, and create a bond with their people through credibility, as well as vulnerability. The attributes of a Renegade Leader are spelled out in the word "renegade" itself:

R – Responsive. They are responsive, resilient, and willing to take responsibility.

E – Energized. They are energized and passionate about their organizations, and they hold a high bar for themselves.

N – No excuses. They accept no excuses and consider failing forward to be better than falling short.

E – Engaged. They are engaged with their people, understand the needs of their customers, and influence the direction of their industries.

G – Growth. They are dedicated to their own growth, as well as the growth of their people and their organization.

A – Achievement and Action. They are achievement and action-oriented. You won't find these leaders only at the end of the conference room table.

D – Decisive. They are quick decision-makers even when a decision is hard to make. Most importantly, their influence expands beyond their four walls.

E – Externally-focused. They care about the success of their people as individuals, the success of their communities, their industries, and the world as a whole.

True Renegade Leaders are a rare breed. They succeed, and so do their companies. Many of the clients I work with are leaders of the pack, out-of-the-box visionaries, gifted, and driven to succeed. Yet, they are missing the key ingredients to getting the outcomes they desire and rightfully deserve—to becoming true Renegade Leaders.

Many of these leaders rush forward in an effort to achieve ultimate success. Naturally, their passion is to succeed. They are people who are meant to make a difference in the world, to stand up, and to be seen and heard. But when they pause for a moment to look behind them, they discover that their staff is lagging behind. It's frustrating. Their message isn't being heard (or worse, it isn't acted upon).

You might know this feeling. You know that success doesn't happen alone, and you know you need your people on board. You need them to buy into your vision, to make it their own and create the thoughts, feelings, and behaviors needed for it to become reality. Here you are with ideas, plans, and a vision you know will work, but when you look over the horizon, you find that your organization, department, or team has taken on a momentum of its own. You might see a huge disconnect between the direction your organization is headed and where you want it to go.

You already know there are all sorts of resources you can put in place to course-correct—leadership training, team building, off-site retreats. But which of these resources will get you the results your organization needs?

Plus, if you're like most leaders, you're probably looking for a solution to the day-to-day management issues that plague you—poor communication; interpersonal conflicts; and lack of engagement, accountability, and teamwork. Some leaders end up working harder to get the results they need from their people. Others react by giving up and retreating while letting the flame of their inner Renegade Leader quietly extinguish.

Working harder won't help you succeed, and retreating is not an option. Your passion runs too deep, your flame cannot be extinguished, and your vision is too important not to materialize.

Without knowing the secrets to becoming a true Renegade Leader, there are three roadblocks that bring most driven leaders to a screeching halt:

1. Ineffective leadership. This is leadership that has not evolved with the times, doesn't work with today's workforce, and no longer produces results.

2. Lack of high performing teams. This results in low accountability, lack of cohesion among team members, and reduced commitment to organizational goals.

3. Organizational cultures that don't provide what employees need to succeed. This breeds lack of employee engagement, hostility, and reduced loyalty.

The Secret Ingredient

The goal of *The Renegade Leader* is to help you break through these roadblocks to better business performance through a secret ingredient: *Influence*. I sifted through all of the research and the solutions I have used with my own clients and deciphered it into nine key attributes. Each chapter in this book is devoted to one of the letters that forms the acronym, I.N.F.L.U.E.N.C.E. As a whole, this acronym is a Framework that offers you a roadmap for igniting people, performance, and profits.

Through applying the attributes of this Framework, you will:

1. Discover how to motivate today's workforce and how to have your message heard and acted upon. Chapters two, three, and four offer competencies that help you become the kind of leader others want to follow.

2. Activate the key employee engagement drivers so that employees easily align with your vision and commit to the overall success of your organization. Chapters five, six, and seven will help you activate the highest performance in your team members.

3. Learn how to build a culture that is steeped in collaboration, creativity, and innovation. Chapters eight, nine, and ten take your culture into the 21st century.

Think about it: How would your professional life change if your teams were as invested in the growth and success of your company as you are? Instead of having to nag, coax, and intimidate indifferent employees into performing their duties (which never works, by the way), you'd finally take your place as the leader of committed individuals collaborating toward the creation of a company culture that inspires innovative thinking and optimizes productivity. And you'd be able to do this without resistance, in a way that is enjoyable and easy for both you and your employees.

If you are looking for buy-in from your staff; a sense of understanding; a "Roger-that" communication that they have listened, comprehended, and are ready, willing, and able to be by your side on the critical road of success, this book will show you the way. Just as seasoned pilots use a checklist before they take flight, consider *The Renegade Leader* to be a checklist to evaluate your organization.

Within the chapters, I have woven a business fable about a fictional CEO named Jim Saunders, allowing you to follow his experience as he implements the I.N.F.L.U.E.N.C.E Framework within his organization. My hope is that this fable will illustrate the main points of *The Renegade Leader* and give you a clearer picture as to how you can use these strategies in your own company.

I encourage you to try on what you learn in each chapter, and alter it to make it your own. This is not a book to remain on the shelf. It gives you immediate access to groundbreaking tools and strategies that help you minimize—and even eliminate—challenges. It is meant for you to take action, use the ideas, and make a difference.

In order to create transformation from the information provided, use the Forward Actions list at the end of each chapter to adapt the behaviors needed for success. For additional success Accelerators, visit our resource site at www.TheRenegadeLeader.com.

Sound good? Then, let's get started!

Chapter 1

Leadership: An Endless Exercise in Steering Corrections

"Leadership and learning are indispensable to each other." -John F. Kennedy

After returning from a meeting with his management team, Jim rubbed his forehead, and felt a headache coming on. It had been one of those days. For the past two years, he had served as CEO of McClarkson Consulting, a large consulting firm with seven offices. Getting to this place had not been easy. He joined the company as a manager and, within five years, started to really see its potential.

Back then, McClarkson was a small consulting firm just outside of Washington, D.C. Owned by Frank O'Malley, it focused on providing web-based technology for accounting, contract management, and client relationship management.

Frank had done a great job building relationships and gaining enough business to more than keep the company afloat. He thought of McClarkson as a small, "cater to your every need" service business.

Jim, on the other hand, didn't see the company as small at all. He knew it could be much larger, expansive, and well-known, and he wanted to implement a standard of service that left their competitors behind. He could taste the potential. So, when Jim learned that Frank was thinking about retiring, he stepped forward and declared he felt ready to take over as owner.

Frank had always admired Jim. He was young and ambitious just like Frank had been at that age. Jim was an enthusiastic man who was married with a family; he had high integrity and shared Frank's values.

But liking Jim didn't mean Frank was going to just hand over the company. After all, he had built this baby from scratch. He wanted to make sure he left a legacy behind that continued to thrive. He would want to give Jim some guidance, and besides, he couldn't imagine himself retired, passing time with his wife every day while he wondered how the business was doing. The staff was like his extended family, and he needed to still be "in the know."

It took six long months of negotiation, but Jim and Frank finally worked out an agreement. They decided on a one-year transition. Just in case the ship started to sink during that time, Frank would still be around enough to jump in and save it. Satisfied, Frank left after a send-off party, feeling proud of the legacy he was leaving behind.

Jim was relieved, but he was chomping at the bit to move into the big office where he could begin to paint his own colors on the company canvas. The day he slid into the CEO chair, he knew he had always owned it. He itched to fulfill his dream of growing the company. He wanted and deserved to be at the front of the line, known as the best both by his customers and the industry.

But he had to quiet himself. After all, there was a little something called a one-year transition agreement. Luckily, Jim had always been a take control kind of guy, so it wasn't difficult to keep the company humming at its usual momentum during the first year of his tenure as CEO. Some of the staff members seemed a bit resistant at first, and others complained for months that his way was "not how they did it before." So, Jim paced himself, making his changes gradually and trying to stick with the status quo for the most part. But he was just biding his time.

He also didn't mind the occasional visits from Frank and always found that his predecessor had something to offer, even when they disagreed. Whenever he didn't like one of Frank's suggestions, he simply nodded respectfully, knowing he was going to do things his way anyway. By the time the first year came to a close, Frank's visits had become less frequent.

All seemed to be going reasonably well, but Jim was far from satisfied, of course. He began to make plans for growth and had secret conversations with others in his industry that he purposely did not share with Frank or anyone else in the company. Once the transition year had passed, he was ready to make his move.

Jim had an opportunity to merge with another midsized consulting firm, Rumbletree Advisors, located in Phoenix, Arizona. Rumbletree's clients extended all the way to the West Coast. The problem was that the company had fallen under poor leadership due to the personal health issues of its CEO, and operations mismanagement had caused implementation delays. As a result, some of its clients were no longer what you'd call raving fans. While it still had a lot going for it, the company had become shaky and vulnerable, and the CEO wanted out. After several phone calls and meetings, Rumbletree's absentee owner was impressed with Jim and happy to talk about a merger.

Meanwhile, Jim had been storing away reserves gained by his streamlined cost control and precision operations, and he felt that the services and products Rumbletree offered would be a nice complement to McClarkson's. Rumbletree's small team of employees seemed very knowledgeable, and Jim felt there would be little need for staffing adjustments.

Jim still thought of Frank as a mentor, so when he finally revealed his plan to his predecessor, he was pleased that Frank offered his blessing. Soon, both organizations came to a pending financial agreement, and Jim was excited to unveil the news to his extended management team.

Jim called a meeting, preparing for it like an honors student. He was armed with spreadsheets, financial projections, client lists, and an implementation plan. He knew who would do what and by when. He prided himself on how well his intuitive knowledge always seemed to work for him. Smiling like a Cheshire cat, he could hardly contain himself as he entered the room for the meeting.

Jim shared the financial data and projections, and he expressed his confidence in the team's ability to make the transition happen easily. He was so focused on his presentation, though, that he failed to notice the tension in the air and the baffling glances exchanged among his people.

After three hours of trying to get his team excited about the expansion, all they had to offer were questions, concerns, and roadblocks. He had at least expected his consulting manager, Paul, to have a positive idea or two. Surely, he saw the potential in expanding client services. Nothing.

Peggy, the sales manager, who should have seen the potential of positioning themselves more competitively, only balked at the idea, stating that her team already had too much competition for few sales. "Why would we want to bring on internal competition as well?" she asked.

The most motivated person in the room was the youngest team member, Sheila, who shared a few thoughts but offered no structure to her ideas. They simply fell like raindrops on the table, quickly evaporating in the heat of the stuffy conference room.

"Why aren't you getting it?" Jim almost said aloud. He was frustrated with their questions and wondered why he had to justify his decision at all.

It wasn't the first time Jim had felt like this. Sometimes, he was so angry that he felt like firing all of them and starting all over again. Why was his team so resistant to anything new? Their heads were so stuck in the minutia of day-to-day tasks that they were blinded to the big picture.

And his managers were the worst. He wondered if they were ever going to have the guts to make their own decisions or really be part of the company's future. Sometimes, he felt alone as a leader. Why couldn't they step up to the plate now and then?

"I hate meetings anyway," Jim said to himself in a huff. "Most are a waste of time. Sometimes, everybody seems more interested in their lattés or dunkachinos than in what I'm saying."

One thing was for sure, though. Jim couldn't accomplish this expansion without them. His neck reddened as he felt his anger well up inside him. "I don't need their approval," he told himself finally. "I'll just decide, and they'll have to live with my decision. It's either that, or be gone."

A heated sea of negativity washed over him. Although his teams were productive, he knew they could do so much more. He thought of the day-to-day dramas, the interpersonal conflicts, the wasted time, and the gross lack of accountability. He was determined to make changes. Nothing was going to hold him back. That merger was happening, and he was in charge, steering the way. Everyone else had better just damn well get on board.

You Can't Steer a Parked Car

Do you think Jim's plan will work? Can he force his team to follow what he demands? Unfortunately, what Jim intends to do is a bit like trying to steer a parked car. As long as it's parked, the car's make, model, or potential for high performance don't matter. And just like a car, an organization can't move unless it is ignited. Then, once started, it can't keep up its endurance without the right fuel and maintenance.

Jim is hardly an unusual case. Many leaders are struggling today. They don't seem to be as effective anymore, or their people don't seem to be as responsive. Direct orders no longer go unquestioned, and few teams leave a conference room ready to get into action. Instead, people ask why, demand information, and seek answers before committing themselves to anything new.

Change occurs at an accelerated rate today. Think of the technology you've added to your life: You carry thousands of songs in your pocket, your computer is as thin as your portfolio, a world of information is at your fingertips, and you have "friends" from around the world via social networking. It really shouldn't come as a surprise that your people have grown and changed as well. They have different needs than the employees of the past.

Today's employees are smarter, more innovative, more creative, and full of potential. Many grew up with technology and thrive on a sense of community. Social contacts are just as important as family members, even more so for younger generations. Unlike team members of earlier generations, today's workers like the feel of collaboration and want to be actively involved in any decisions that affect their work.

Many leaders, no matter how long they've been at it, are unsure how to manage these 21st century employees. They wonder what style of leadership is most effective. The key words "leadership style" were searched on Google by hundreds of thousands of people this month alone. As you might suspect, the old top-down style of leadership no longer works. "Management-centered" or "command and control" models of leadership have been proven to breed a lack of accountability and creativity, increased resentment, and poor outcomes.

As a result of these leadership methods, performance is on the decline. In many organizations, everyone appears to be busy, but not a lot is getting done. Staff members are accountable only if others get them what they need by when they need it, and work is done only if employees believe it's important, even though it may be critical from management's point of view.

What are these old styles? Here are some of the strategies of the past that are now ineffective:

- Borrowing position from title: "I'm the boss" or "because I said so."

- Fear tactics; threatening to terminate an employee or take away future promotions/benefits.

- Managing people as human capital versus honoring them as emotional beings.

- Trying to motivate with financial rewards that only offer short-term returns.

The Dismal Employee Engagement Picture

Are these antiquated leadership styles standing in the way of employee engagement in your organization? An engaged employee is defined as one who arrives at work striving for excellence and focuses on the overall success of their employer. How many of your employees can you say that about?

Would it surprise you to learn that if yours is like most companies, only 27% of your employees are engaged? According to the U.S. results from the Towers Perrin's Global Workforce Study titled "Closing the Engagement Gap: A Roadmap for Driving Superior Business Performance," there is a direct link between employee engagement and business performance. Looking at the statistics, you will see why.

If only 27% of employees are engaged, what are the others doing? In a company of 100 employees, only 27 show up daily, loyal to the company and committed to doing their best work; 59 are not engaged; and 14 just show up—they don't really care. They simply pass time on your dime.

In addition, 77 report feeling burned out, 33 say they are overworked, 67 feel overwhelmed, 7 are sinking into deep depression, and 50 are open to switching jobs if another becomes available. It doesn't paint a very pretty picture, does it?

With only some of your staff productive, you can imagine the cost to your organization. Disengagement costs an estimated $240-$270 billion a year in lost productivity. The Conference Board on Employee Engagement reports that there is a direct correlation between employee engagement and desirable business outcomes, such as retention of talent, customer service, individual performance, team performance, business unit productivity, and even enterprise-level financial performance. What might this problem be costing you?

And this disease is leading to the decline of many organizations.

In 2001, Jim Collins wrote *Good to Great,* which profiled 60 growing companies. In his new book, *How the Mighty Fall and Why Some Companies Never Give In*, he reveals why many of the same companies eventually deteriorated and disappeared. Let's take a look at the bigger picture.

A full one-third of the companies listed in the 1970 Fortune 500 had vanished by 1983 (they were out of business, acquired, merged, or broken into pieces). Every ten years, one of three major companies fails, and on average, Fortune 500 companies last only 30-50 years. Sun, Digital Equipment Corporation, and General Motors did not survive. These were companies that had money, political clout, and alliances to endure, but they didn't.

What went wrong? There is accumulating evidence that corporations fail because their prevailing focus is on revenues, reducing costs, and improving operations. Of course, you recognize these functions as the arterial system of your organization. But what creates the pulse of the organization, feeds all of its roadways, and makes it sustainable? *The people who work for you.*

Without the commitment from your people, little success can be had, growth is difficult, and your competitors easily advance forward, leaving you in the dust. Today's successful leaders, in addition to having a mission statement and a strategic plan, also develop a roadmap for the success and engagement of their people.

The Secret to Sustainability

In an effort to determine what makes organizations sustainable, Shell Corporation funded the Long Lived Company Study. This study determined key components of longevity after assessing companies that were 200 or more years old. The study revealed that these companies saw themselves as a community first and a profit center second. Their cultures had a sense of identity and shared values. They focused on culture—a way of "being" that promoted success—and their culture was reflected in their processes and systems, as well as how they interacted with employees, customers, stakeholders, and their community at large. There was a tolerance and openness, and everyone shared in fiscal awareness and social consciousness.

We hear the term "culture" bandied about, but what does it really mean? Culture is defined as a shared belief system of values and processes within an organization. It has been described simply as "the way we do things." It is a powerful component to any organization and has both explicit and implicit characteristics.

Corporate culture is a philosophy to guide organizational strategy, workforce behavior, and management attitudes. Leadership is considered the key element for defining and driving workplace culture. Through your leadership style, you can shape and develop your company's culture in the same way you develop sales, operations, or marketing. It all begins with you.

What can you do to ensure your organization's sustainability? Renegade Leadership is the beginning. Creating a culture that resonates with the 21st century workforce ensures your ability to lead others with certainty. This type of leadership requires heavy work: laying down the foundations of trust; building the pillars of shared values, allowing collaboration and joint leadership; and making room for transparent communication and innovation.

While information is nice, what you really want is transformation. Past decades were about the "doing" of leadership and organizational development. Today's leader focuses on the "being" of leadership—being the leader others model, creating a culture of leadership, and being the leader who invigorates the highest performance in the individuals he/she oversees.

Give Your People What They Want

Transformation is a big word, but how do you accomplish it in the real day-to-day world of a functioning company? The Towers Perrin's Global Workforce Study and the latest employee engagement studies indicate that there are ten drivers of employee engagement that impact business results. Look at the list below, and assess how well you, your organization, and your employees rate in these key areas:

1. Senior management's sincere interest in employee well-being.

2. Opportunities to improve skills and capabilities.

3. The organization's reputation for social responsibility.

4. Opportunities to provide input into decision-making in the employee's department.

5. The organization's ability to quickly resolve customer concerns.

6. An individual employee's own readiness to set high personal standards.

7. Excellent career advancement opportunities.

8. An individual employee's interest in challenging work assignments.

9. Employees' relationship with supervisors.

10. The organization's willingness to encourage innovative thinking.

The I.N.F.L.U.E.N.C.E. Framework was designed with these attributes in mind and offers you the roadmap and leadership incentives to get everyone on board, in the right seats, facing in the right direction, and ready to move forward.

This "people-centered" style of management is what leads to greater success. This approach means relinquishing control to others and trusting that employees will not abuse that responsibility. You steer but allow your people to drive. For many leaders, this is not easy to do; it takes confidence to pull it off.

But when you read the following attributes of engaged employees, you can see that the payoffs are well worth it:

• Able to perform at the peak of their potentials.

• Connected to the company and its vision.

• Motivated to go above and beyond perfunctory performance.

• Responsible concerning their role in the company.

• Passionate about the success of the company and the actions they can take to ensure that success.

Where the Rubber Meets the Road

The effects of people-centered leadership on your bottom line are eye-opening. Performance isn't the only thing that soars; profits also soar. With increased engagement, teams function better, tasks are performed with ease, little time is wasted, and there is greater commitment to improving the bottom line in all areas.

The executives and business owners who become exemplary Renegade Leaders all gain an increase in both performance and profits. My company has even seen clients double their profits.

CFO magazine reports that Best Buy experiences a $100,000 increase in net operating income for every tenth of a point increase in employee engagement. What would happen if you simply moved your employees' level of engagement by just a fraction?

The MGM Grand focused on employee engagement and noted an annual benefit in increased operating profits over the last five-year period. Zappos built a culture based on happiness—delivering happiness to its customers and creating a fun place to work that allows its employees to be spontaneous and creative and to have a say in decisions. Its unprecedented customer service caught the eye of Amazon, which purchased Zappos in 2010.

What might be possible for your organization? Leadership doesn't have to be difficult. If you are feeling stalled or frustrated like Jim that you aren't moving as fast as you desire or aren't getting the results you expected, don't worry; high performance is just around the corner.

Take the Renegade Leader challenge, and try on the strategies outlined in the I.N.F.L.U.E.N.C.E. Framework. Let's add your story to the success stories of other leaders my company has worked with:

- Julie was president of her organization, and she dreamed of being the best in performance. Her vision was to expand her company from the East Coast to the West and to take her rightful place as a recognized leader in her industry. She loved building relationships with business partners, prospects, and clients, and she focused on serving her customers. She believed her people should know how to do their jobs and be capable of working independently. Therein was the pothole in her plan: Her team needed her to provide direction. They needed to know where they were going and what they were expected to do to get there. No matter what Julie did, her company seemed to stay in the slow lane—that is until she activated a new style of leadership. Once she shared the vision, and she and her executive team defined their core values and turned them into daily behaviors, she was able to expand her business nationally. Leadership was fostered at many levels, allowing her the time to identify and merge easily with other organizations. This freed time for her to do what she loved best: Be with her customers and make a mark in her industry. Through the process of altering her leadership style, Julie's dream had come true.

- Tim fantasized about having a unified company. My firm helped him to negotiate a buyout of his long-term partners and create his vision for the company's future. After learning about employee engagement and the challenges of other workplaces, Tim committed himself to a people-focused strategy plan. We worked together to define the culture that would support his vast vision, asking his management team to determine the cultural values that would help them achieve company goals. Tim then invested in his people, and my firm provided leadership training and coaching competencies to his management team. While many of the businesses in his industry were gravely impacted by the economy, Tim's profits grew by 50 percent within the year, and within two years, his growth was six times the national average for his industry. Combined with streamlined operations and leadership excellence, this allowed the company to open up a new business concept within a year, employing 100 people in our community.

- Ariel accelerated her pace as a new vice president of multiple divisions and gained the recognition of her national non-profit organization. She knew that she needed freedom from day-to-day management in order to achieve her goals, but the day-to-day drama of leadership was holding her down, while her division experienced the high cost of turnover. The solution was to understand what her people needed to be successful and foster greater leadership within her team members. She gathered her multiple division heads and formed a goal-oriented focus group. Ariel learned to trust her team members to lead effectively, and her new leadership skills served as the model for others. The department worked together in collaboration, and the vibration shifted to renewed energy and positivity. With leaders at all levels, Ariel has been able to take on greater fiscal responsibilities and determine what new programs and services will best serve the company's clients.

- Charlie was rising in the ranks, but he was told that he needed to take care of the interpersonal conflicts that existed in his department, as well as the lack of collaboration during team meetings. When he focused on nourishing trust, he quickly discovered why his teams were not communicating in meetings. With my firm's help, he developed a plan for professional development that focused on open communication. As a result, conversations flourished, interpersonal conflicts were resolved, and employee engagement soared.

- Joe confessed that even though he was a CEO, he hated the "messy people part" of the job. It was no surprise that his people floundered without direction, and they lacked accountability. Using a few key leadership strategies, he was able to gain commitment and respect from his team, and his objectives were met with ease.

Like you, perhaps, all of these leaders had a vision and simply needed a roadmap to get there. As I said, you can't steer a parked car, and too many organizations are stalled right now.

You also can't win the race with a lower performance vehicle or with leadership that is not tuned to today's calibrations.

See what Jim discovers when he uses the principles of the I.N.F.L.U.E.N.C.E. Framework to inspire his people to get on board and join him in the winners circle.

Chapter 2

❚NFLUENCE

Inspire Leadership:
Creating the Spark

"Outstanding leaders go out of their way to boost the self-esteem of their people. If people believe in themselves, it's amazing what they can accomplish." –Sam Walton, founder of Wal-Mart

Jim arrived home from his team meeting in an exasperated mood. He was happy to discover that his wife, Julie, was at an evening meeting, so he could eat dinner alone while mulling over the past year in his mind. He had done a good job managing the company, as the financial spreadsheets proved, but he wondered if he could manage his people better. Was there a way to get them as excited about his vision for the company as he felt?

His team relied on him, but he was tired of having to be the parent in the room. He wanted so much more than that. Why did he have to explain every little thing, offering bite-sized portions in order for them to digest the information? Had it been the same for Frank? Jim felt the tension in his neck muscles, which was where he always carried the stress of business. It was exhausting.

Before going to bed, Jim emptied his briefcase of the odds and ends collected from the day: phone messages, reminder notes for active projects, and the receipt for the large grilled Panini he had for lunch (something Julie would frown upon). There in the stack of papers, notebooks, and folders (which seemed urgent enough to bring home at six o'clock but less urgent to review by ten o'clock) was a document he had downloaded and printed from the Internet. The title had intrigued him: The I.N.F.L.U.E.N.C.E. Framework: How to Get the Business Results You Want with the People and Resources You Already Have.

He had been receiving a weekly briefing, "Unlock Your Personal Power of Influence," from the same author and was invited in a recent email to receive the longer document. Jim wasn't a big reader; it wasn't even like him to download anything. But he had enjoyed some of the weekly briefings, and like most leaders, he was always looking for ways to be more strategic. So, he decided to take a look at the document as he got into bed.

Upon her return, Julie noticed Jim's dim mood, so she quietly began reading one of her novels. This was probably a good thing because Jim was still tense from the day's events, and he knew that his stress sometimes spilled over into his relationships.

As he read the beginning of the Framework, Jim wondered if he was an "influential leader." What did that really mean? "I'm driven," he thought, "and I've always enjoyed working. And I'm very competitive. I get into the fun of the game, and I like to play hard and win. I get a kick out of negotiating and driving home the deal, but I also try to make sure everyone feels whole about it." He brushed the hair off his face. "I like being in charge, but I wish I wasn't the go-to person for everything. I'll bet everybody else from work is at home relaxing and reading novels right now like Julie."

Sighing out his disappointment and agitation, Jim soon became engrossed in reading about the I.N.F.L.U.E.N.C.E. Framework. He was nearly halfway through when Julie yawned and asked how much longer he was going to stay up. He grabbed his robe and slippers and made his way to the living room, disturbing his small dog's deep slumber on his way out the door to the living room couch.

As Jim continued reading, he began to see how his leadership style had been failing him. The words leapt off the page:

- *Leading with influence.*

- *Fostering leadership at all levels.*

- *Collaboration.*

- *Growth.*

- *Accountability.*

- *Engaged employees.*

- *Increased productivity.*

- *Higher profits.*

- *Work/life balance.*

Could he really have it all with the people and resources he already had?

For the first time, Jim truly understood the challenge he was up against. The employee engagement statistics were eye-opening; no wonder most organizations were in trouble. He was encouraged, however, when he read that 41% of the disengaged could be "re-enrolled" by activating employee engagement drivers. Still, he was surprised to learn that the relationship with senior management was the top employee engagement driver.

It was becoming clear as he continued reading: McClarkson hadn't evolved with the times. It had been some time since they offered employees an opportunity to improve skills, and their lack of emphasis on the needs of individuals was clear. Jim had followed in Frank's shoes, only sharing what was needed when it was needed. Although he did take an active interest in every department, he failed to take that interest to the employee level. Frank had been more personally engaged with each member of the staff.

"But I'm CEO! Do I really have to do that?" he wondered. "Well, I guess I've been so focused on the destination toward the merger that I haven't done the work to get people on board. And the company as it stands right now isn't strong enough to expand, not without re-enrolling everyone to their highest performance. Maybe then, they'll be more open to the idea of growth."

Like most Renegade Leaders, Jim cared about his employees. They were well paid, and bonuses were provided with increased profitability. What he hadn't recognized was that his employees needed to know why decisions were being made. They needed a voice at the big table and a say in the tone of the company's direction. Sure, they didn't appear to have this desire, but after reading the Framework, Jim was aware he hadn't actually invited them to engage in this way.

"If I do this right, I can quickly unite the two companies and have everyone feel a part of the same family," Jim thought with renewed excitement. The Framework began by detailing how inspired leaders, who are few and far between, are the most capable of creating high performing organizations. "Many leaders are able to provide focus, direction, and a strategic plan," Jim read, "but it takes an inspired leader to translate vision and values into active behaviors, to develop milestones and benchmarks, and to inspire others to execute the vision successfully. Inspiration promotes innovation, and innovative companies are the ones that make the cover of Fortune magazine." That's the kind of leader Jim wanted to be.

He realized that he could be more inspired and that pushing the merger had not helped matters. His desperation to get the merger done quickly had quieted other voices from talking about it. He had cast anyone who was against the merger as his enemy—as someone preventing him from achieving his goals.

"Be the light that ignites others," the I.N.F.L.U.E.N.C.E. Framework said. Jim had paused when he read that. Had he ever been that? Or did his presence overshadow the brightest light of some individuals? Did his unwillingness to listen often blow out the candle of someone else's brilliant idea?

Implementing the I.N.F.L.U.E.N.C.E. Framework offered an opportunity to grow, maintain a competitive edge, and ensure the sustainability of the company. After all, Jim was a numbers man; statistics made sense to him. He could cite the company's financials as well as he knew his name. And the statistics in the Framework were too compelling to ignore: Sixty-eight percent of engaged employees want a stake in reducing costs and improving the bottom line, and 72 percent believe they can create a positive impact on service delivery and client retention. Engaged employees perform 30 percent more than disengaged ones, and 84 percent of them remain loyal to the company. Who wouldn't want to reduce the high cost of turnover? Jim had to admit that these were impressive numbers.

More importantly, he knew that not everyone fared well with change. He didn't want to lose the talent the company had accrued over the years. "With the merger, creating shared values is going to be even more important, and I need everyone to play 'all in' in order to win the game," he said aloud to himself.

Yes, as he thought about the criteria for the Framework and how to influence people, ignite performance, and impact profits, he knew things had to change. First, he needed to adopt the new leadership mindset by exploring it and making it his own. Then, he could activate an employee engagement strategy that focused on the culture that the Framework promised. As much as he had been chomping at the bit to get the merger completed, he was now chomping at the bit to become a more effective Renegade Leader. The first step of the Framework was to activate inspiration, to inspire others, and to be more inspiring himself.

His heart raced; if he could do this I.N.F.L.U.E.N.C.E. thing, he could get the merger done. People would get excited about it. He could feel it. He scribbled a stack of notes until just past one o'clock. Reenergized and planning to go to work early, he reset his alarm and went to sleep, having a deeper rest than he had experienced in a long time.

Becoming an Inspired and Inspiring Leader

How do you think Jim will do with his newfound realizations? It's going to take some work to change, isn't it? Habits are hard to break. You probably drive to work on the same route every day, hardly noticing what it takes to arrive. You might be leading the same way as well, in a rut of blind repetition. But what if leadership was a new adventure, like test driving a race car? What if you could own the road, blast between lanes, maneuver with controlled precision, and experience a laugh loosening from your throat in a voice you might not even recognize as your own? Which sounds like more fun?

A common denominator of successful leaders is inspiration. These are leaders who are energized and passionate. Through their own vibration, they cause a ripple effect of inspiration in others. As Donald Trump once said, "If you don't have passion, you have no energy, and if you don't have energy, you have nothing. It all starts with passion."

As an expert in psychology and an avid researcher in the field of neuroscience (the study of the human nervous system, the brain, and the biological basis of consciousness, perception, memory, and learning), I know that the emotional mood in an organization mirrors the emotions of its leaders. So, take a moment now to check in with yourself. How excited are you about the work you do? How much energy do you have? How positive are you about your organization, its people, and its purpose? Where do you rate in energy, passion, and positivity?

So many of my new clients tell me they are exhausted and overwhelmed by leadership. Others claim their inner Renegade Leader "has been beaten out of them by the system." True Renegade Leaders often have such an intensity of passion that it sometimes leaves them short-tempered when their employees don't share the same exuberance. Some confuse inspiration with friendship and are surprised when team members who are their friends don't produce results. Others create inspired teams but fail to harness and direct the energy. What type of leader are you?

Jim is certainly inspired. He has a vision that he dreams about, he loves his work, and he's confident. But now, he needs to learn how to get others as inspired as he is about the merger. Then, once successful, he must discover how to inspire the two newly merged organizations to become one.

With all of the challenges facing today's workforce, John Zenger and Joseph Folkman, the authors of the book, *Extraordinary Leaders*, reveal 16 competencies that separate top leaders from the rest. The consensus of the research indicates that there is one key ingredient needed for a leader to succeed.

That ingredient is—you guessed it—inspiration, which is defined as "stimulation of the mind or emotions to a high level of feeling or activity."

If you lead in any capacity, you are the spark that ignites others. You hold the key. You are the one who starts the engines and turns over the organization in the morning. Through your direction, you help your teams determine the destination, draft the course, and calculate the speed of arrival. Do you inspire your organization to go from 0 to 60, or does it merely sputter along?

One of my favorite books is *Delivering Happiness* by CEO Tony Hsieh. His leadership at Zappos and that of his managers and employees truly aligns with the principles of the I.N.F.L.U.E.N.C.E Framework, starting with inspired leadership.

Inspiration is not just a "nice to have" quality. It is a skill and a talent that yields a serious return on investment. Bottom line: Leaders who inspire outperform those who don't. Unfortunately, only one in ten employees reports that their leader is inspired and inspirational. It's not surprising when you think about it.

Traditional leadership used to be about efficiency. Since we learned about the seven habits of effective people, leaders have focused on doing things and accomplishing projects, timelines, and results. A good leader has the capacity to meet a goal on time and preferably under budget. A great leader, however, produces results and, at the same time, enjoys working with his/her team, builds great relationships, and empowers each team member. How do you go from good to great?

Take a closer look at inspirational leaders you know, and you'll see that the ability to inspire is a bit more clear-cut than you thought. That's not to say it's easy, but when you look closely at what makes a leader inspirational, you'll realize there's no secret or magic to it.

The Difference Between Average and Inspired

Just like average leaders, inspired leaders have the skills, experience, education, background, and knowledge to understand the business and what's needed for its success. But unlike average leaders, inspired leaders realize it's just as important to focus on the values, passions, and unique skills of each employee as it is to focus on the everyday tasks at hand. They take the time to find out what's meaningful to their employees, and they structure their employees' work so that meaning and purpose are fulfilled.

Think back to a time when you felt inspired. What did that feel like? Chances are, you felt like the job you had or the role you were playing within the organization was a dead-on match with your unique skills, passions, and drives. Your job was meaningful to you, so you were deeply invested in it. Your leader put you in a position to be your very best and consistently recognized the positive impact you were having on the organization. How did he or she do this? Simply by showing you how your job was important and that your contribution was valued. Once that connection is made, an employee is almost unstoppable.

Inspiration is intentional. Leaders have the ability to inspire if they have a handle on their attitude and are willing to invest the time and effort to get to know their employees. Inspiration is about focusing as much energy, drive, and commitment to help your employees feel successful as it is filling your days with business strategies, vision statements, and financial planning.

It's about creating a culture and environment that vibrates with possibility and creativity.

So, how do you get started? The first step to inspiring others is to be inspired yourself. You won't be able to implement the I.N.F.L.U.E.N.C.E Framework if you don't have the capacity to lead with inspiration, and it's impossible to create a movement of inspired, engaged employees unless you are committed to your own success and engaged in your own work, life, learning, and business. Make sure your health, spirit, and drive are maintained before you ask others to get on board. Ponder what shifts you need to make to get yourself in gear, to have the drive to move forward, and to be committed to accelerating your results.

What could you do to make your work more fulfilling? What vision have you not yet explored? Where are you playing small versus all-in? As Jim will learn, you inspire others when you show up as your authentic self, vulnerabilities and all.

Once you have inspired yourself, focus on your teams. They don't need to be groomed every moment with the warm glove of inspiration, but they do need to see that you are inspired—that you see the possibility in them, in the organization, in your products and services, and in your business, especially at times when they feel their backs are against the wall. Inspired leaders focus on and value the strengths and contributions of their employees so that everyone takes pride in their work.

When you focus on who your employees are, you let them know the company cares about them and their well-being. This creates an emotional bond between workers and the organization, and there's nothing like an emotional bond to ensure that employees give their absolute most. They are then attached to their jobs, their company, their customers, and even to you. Inspiration is what drives employees to perform; it is the root of employee engagement.

FORWARD ACTIONS
Inspiration Starts with You

1. Spend a couple of days looking at your environment, as well as your actions. Do your employees seem excited or overwhelmed? Are they passionate about what they're doing or just going through the motions? Are meetings full of eager employees sharing ideas and thoughts, or do they focus on what's not quite right? When you speak to your employees, do you focus on their unique strengths and passions and how they can contribute to the organization's goals and ultimate success, or do you focus on their weaknesses and mistakes?

2. Focus on people before tasks. Discover the unique strengths, talents, passions, and values of your employees, and find ways that allow them to use this brilliance in their job functions. Ask them what they need to feel successful at the end of the day, and help them to create the work, learning opportunities, and growth that meet those objectives.

3. Share the big vision. Your people are ready for it. It's far from motivating to only see a small part of a big picture. If you're excited, your people will be, too. Let them be part of setting the course for success. They

will be much more committed to a plan of action that they help to create.

4. Let your people know you value their contribution, and help them to understand how important it is to the company. It's disempowering to make a widget on an assembly line without knowing how it fits into the product it helps to produce.

5. Manage with visibility and emotional connection. Don't be afraid to be present, to show up fully, even when you don't know the answers or when the bottom is falling out. You inspire others when you show them you are confident in them, yourself, and your organization to meet the challenges that arise.

6. Model for others what you expect of them. Be an example by living the values you want your organization to exude. If you don't want to waste time on gossip, for example, don't talk about others. If you want people to arrive to meetings on time, don't be late yourself. If you want employees to trust you and be open, allow them space to be heard. Increase your capacity for empathy, listening, and emotional and social intelligence.

7. Self-monitor your own energy. Everyone experiences highs and lows. Know that as a leader, your lows affect the people around you, at work as well as at home. Develop a strategy to shake off the lows, put negative energy aside, and move forward through

these periods. Not only will your people be positively impacted, but you will experience improved health and peace of mind (and so will your family!)

8. Use powerful words to inspire powerful change, such as "reveal," "validate," "motivate," "compel," "elaborate," "assure," "emphasize," "action," "entice," "gain," "optimize," and "leverage." Leave negativity at the threshold, and enter the building as an inspired leader.

To put your results into overdrive, visit our "Inspire Leadership" Accelerators at

www.TheRenegadeLeader.com

Chapter 3
I**N**FLUENCE

Nourish Trust: Gaining Sure-Footed Traction in Your Organization

"Trust is the essence of leadership."—Colin Powell

The next morning, Jim kissed Julie goodbye and breezed out the door, ready to take on the new day. When he arrived at his office in Trilogy Square, he unlocked the oversized double doors. The modern office building had glass with a greenish luster, thus earning its insider name of "the Emerald City." Its marble lobby was an open atrium with plants and seating areas, and the executive offices and conference rooms on all ten floors faced the center. While he liked the openness and Zen-like feel, he didn't like the way the conference rooms were exposed. He hated the confined feeling of closing the heavy drapes to the atrium. There had been many times when Jim felt ill at ease in a staff meeting as he noticed a set of eyes peering through the windows. It stopped him cold one day as he saw someone watching while he yelled at one of his team members. Jim hoped his new plan would mean no more yelling.

This particular day, the office building itself seemed welcoming. The coffee was already brewing in the small deli downstairs, and its aroma lingered in the lobby. Jim entered his waiting room and looked around. Behind the front desk was the company sign, big and bold, solid and grounded, like the company itself. To the right were the sales and consulting offices, and to the left were the row of executive offices: CEO, CFO, and Operations. He noticed the separation for the first time and made a mental note to reorganize the offices.

He looked in his own office, neat as always (other than the stack of project files he kept on his side table). He rarely sat at his desk; his big chair still looked fairly new. Its high back towered invitingly over the desk. Jim, however, liked to roam. He liked to be in the offices of his people, keeping tabs on what was happening, using his quiet office only when he needed to focus.

He noticed the chairs for his visitors, often warmed by the bodies of anxious team members reporting problems and seeking his solutions. The visitor chairs were lower than his chair with thinly covered cloth seats and wooden arms. Jim remembered sitting there many times to talk to Frank and feeling a little bit smaller in status as a result.

A small table, cluttered with mail and industry magazines, was pushed over to the side of the room. No one had sat in the two chairs there for a while. It was like seeing his office for the first time. Jim knew he would have to implement some changes if he was to follow the Framework. "This set-up certainly doesn't inspire trust," he thought.

"My table could become a working area to brainstorm," he began to plan in his head. "The conference room could be given a fun, think tank-type of label, and the executive team's offices could be intertwined with other staff offices. Yeah, an environmental change might shake things up a bit, but that's okay. Nothing happens unless something moves." He paused and looked around. "I wonder what everyone will think of these ideas," he contemplated.

He was warmed by the possibility of it all. Like other Renegade Leaders, Jim was a man of action. When he got an idea, he moved on it, often to the disdain of his management team, who were a bit slower in pace. Usually, by the time he spoke with his managers, he had thought through the idea so deeply that there was no room in his mind for further evaluation.

He knew he had to be careful not to continue in this way even though it came naturally to him. The day before, he had felt angry that the rest of the company didn't trust in his plans for the merger, but the Framework had helped him to come to terms with the fact that they simply needed more information. Perhaps they didn't trust it due to some unanswered questions.

He could understand where they were coming from. He had been attracted to shiny objects before that crashed and burned, making quick decisions that didn't always produce the most positive results. The team just needed to be reassured. He

41

had to pull back the curtain and reveal the vision he had been harboring for months. Then, they needed time to digest the information. "Maybe they could even add some perspectives," he wondered. "After all, this is a huge investment, a big shift for the company, and it means adjustments that will impact everyone. They just aren't convinced yet that it's worth it— that's all."

Jim was ready to see his company through a new lens. The excitement raced through his veins as the staff began to arrive. He watched them enter one by one, coffee in one hand, work materials in the other. Some looked very alert, greeting the receptionist as they walked in, while others looked like they needed a bit more time to wake up. Some of them looked downright exhausted despite the time of day. He saw them as he had never seen them before—as individuals—each with a brilliance of their own.

As soon as everyone settled into their offices or cubicles, Jim called Peggy, his director of sales, and asked her to come see him. Peggy was a loyal employee, she had been with the company for nearly eight years, and Jim liked her style. She was somehow able to juggle relationships with her sales reps while also making the bottom line numbers work. When pushed, she protected her people—even from Jim, if necessary—but he decided that she would no longer need to protect them from him. He could become a leader they wanted to be around, one who motivated them and who connected with their struggles in closing sales, finding new prospects, and competing in a saturated market. No longer would he care only about the numbers, causing some reps to occasionally delay a disappointing report or make an unrealistic forecast in order to avoid his negative reaction.

When Peggy arrived, she had no idea that she was a bit of a guinea pig for Jim. He wanted to try out some of his new insight on her. When she walked into his office, she immediately approached the low chair in front of his desk. "Let's sit at the table," Jim quickly said. The table was free of clutter, and the chairs were pulled forward invitingly.

Peggy was a bit apprehensive and looked at him with an expression of distrust. "This is weird," she thought. "I always sit at the desk. Did I do something wrong?" Then, she became alarmed when the thought crossed her mind that Jim might be getting ready to fire her.

"Peggy, I was thinking about the merger, and I know your team has had some reservations," Jim began.

"Oh, great," Peggy thought. "He's going to tell me to shut everybody up, and that isn't going to be easy."

"Jim," Peggy said aloud, "I think they have some legitimate concerns, and it would help a lot if you could just hear..."

Jim cut her off before she could finish. "Oh, I'm definitely interested in hearing what they have to say," he reassured her. "We need to look at this from all sides, and I want to be aware of their ideas to make sure we have every angle covered. What do you think about having a team meeting to talk about it?"

Peggy tried to read his expression. She hadn't expected him to say anything like that. "What's he playing at?" Peggy thought. "He always makes the final decisions anyway, so why bother?"

Jim sensed her distrust, so he continued, "I know that no one is exactly used to me hearing them out, but let's shake up the status quo. Please let them know that I value them and honestly want to hear their opinions. I'd like for them to present both the pros and the cons, though. Do you think they can prepare for that in order for us to meet next week?"

"Uh ... okay, Jim. That sounds good. I'll ... I'll make it happen," Peggy responded with a look of surprise on her face.

Jim was so accustomed to making all of the bottom line decisions that he felt resistance well up inside him. He knew he had to ignore the sensation, though. Peggy seemed to react positively to his words, and he felt that he was starting to do "this inspired leader thing."

"Well, like any new habit, it'll take getting used to," Jim thought.

As Peggy walked away, she thought, "Gee, I wonder what was in his morning coffee! Whatever it is, I hope he drinks more of it. But he's right about everyone focusing only on the negatives. It will be good for them to look at the pros as well."

Jim lingered at the table for a moment. This felt good. He had acknowledged Peggy and her team and guided her to think about the positive possibilities for the merger. And while it was a little uncomfortable, it didn't feel like work. He left his office, looking for someone else to practice on. When he turned the corner, he overheard a conversation between two of his sales representatives.

"I think we need to meet their pricing to get this deal," Cindy said to Lilliana. Cindy was a fast learner with the company. Within three short years, she had succeeded in gaining a few large accounts and was making her sales numbers, but she seemed to be struggling to expand her sales territory. Jim often wondered what kept her from getting out there and meeting people.

Lilliana didn't seem to buy into Cindy's strategy. "I think you need to go back there and review the proposal. You know the team is going to kill themselves on the implementation at the pricing they have."

"Lilliana is right," Jim thought, "when you undersell, you feel undervalued, and under-bidding a project takes a toll on the entire organization." Jim decided Cindy was avoiding a conversation with someone, or she wouldn't be willing to cut the cost just to get the deal. He pierced his lips, trying to hold back from interrupting the conversation with his opinions. After all, Cindy's manager would have to come to him anyway before a price reduction could be approved, so he would eventually learn how the situation unfolded.

Jim also knew which client Cindy was talking about. Unfortunately, that client had experienced a few glitches in McClarkson's services the previous year when sales reps were reassigned. "I'll bet the client isn't ready to sign a new contract because Cindy hasn't established enough trust with them," he thought. "Has she talked about the issues of the past and reassured them of her best support for the future?" Maybe her manager could guide her in making the sale at the high value investment and gain their trust at the same time.

Jim also wondered why he required final approval of pricing anyway. Wasn't that just an unnecessary delay in the process? Did he not trust his manager to make a financial choice for the company? Would he or someone else have to take Cindy's place to close the account? And how would that appear to the client?

"I wonder how often the managers swoop in and do the work for our employees because of a lack of trust," he thought. "Even Peggy insists on going on all sales calls when they're nearing a contract, and this is probably because she thinks her salesperson can't close the deal. Wow, that can't feel good to her team." Putting himself in the salesperson's shoes, he would want the glory of the finale, sealing the deal, and arriving back in the office with contract in hand. It probably felt disabling to suddenly have to call in the big dogs. To the client, it undoubtedly appeared as if the salesperson wasn't able to do the job. How could the client then trust the salesperson to provide support? What if the installation went wrong or the technology didn't work, and the manager wasn't available to fix it? Suddenly, Jim could clearly see how lack of trust could cause a customer to buy from someone else.

"Plus, if Peggy's out on a sales call, she isn't available to think about her department at its highest level," Jim realized. Her time could definitely better be used in identifying organizations that are a good fit for the company's products and services, creating great branding messages that easily set her sales team apart from their competitors, taking on proactive fiscal

responsibility, and watching the numbers to make sure they stay on the incline.

Jim began to remember what he had read in the I.N.F.L.U.E.N.C.E. Framework about the issue of trust. He had often told his salespeople to build a foundation of trust with clients, but he hadn't thought much about the importance of building trust between himself, his managers, and his employees. According to the Framework, trust could get his company through difficult times, such as missed installation dates, unexpected costs, technology challenges, and glitches in services.

"Do my employees trust me?" he asked himself. "Peggy didn't seem to when she first arrived in my office this morning. And have I entrusted my managers with enough responsibility to ensure their success?" He had to answer no, but he was determined to change that. "Trust is like a prism," he had read in the Framework. "You have to look at it from all angles. You have to evaluate how you rate on the trust scale from all perspectives—in-house, as well as with clients, lenders, and within your industry."

Jim's thoughts turned to his grown daughter, and he came to the realization that most of their confrontations had been about trust ... or, rather, a lack of trust. He hadn't trusted her to make the right decisions while at a school far away. "What if I had helped her instead to make decisions of the highest integrity?" he thought.

The Framework was serving as a mirror for Jim, and he wasn't 100% proud of what he saw. Could lack of trust be a stumbling block in his organization? If they didn't have enough trust now, how were they supposed to establish it with the newly merged company?

What if he shared his criteria for decision-making? Would Cindy be able to come to the same conclusions as he or her manager?

"This is a big one," he said to himself, "but it's time to look for the cracks in the company's trust foundation and develop a strategy to fill those cracks."

Trust is Your Foundation

It isn't easy to trust that others will make the right decisions and take the same actions you would take. Like many CEOs, Jim's perspective of the company was through a lens even his managers wouldn't have been able to comprehend. He was frequently the only person who understood all of the elements that led to a decision.

Jim plans to look for cracks in his company's trust foundation. He could look for some of the following symptoms of lack of trust. Do you have these in your organization as well?

- Resistance to change

- Sabotage and hiding behaviors

- Negative attitudes

- Finger pointing and lack of accountability

- Complaining and focusing on problems rather than solutions

- Complaints about the management team

- Heightened emotions

- Risk avoidance

- Employee turnover

If you aren't careful, these symptoms can spread like a virus of distrust throughout your organization.

Why care about trust? The Elderman Trust Barometer is a global survey that revealed some important statistics in 2010: Employees trust information from peers, industry analysts, and academics more than they trust information from their CEO. The study also discovered that less than 30 percent of people surveyed in the United States believed their CEO was credible.

What would happen if your employees didn't trust you or the other leaders in your organization? How effective could they be? How committed would they be to their work, your customers, and your success? In recent years, starting with the Enrons of the world, employees have lost their trust. Now, more than ever, it is important to assess if trust is an attribute that warrants your attention.

Jim was surprised that his team was resistant to the merger, but the truth is that inconsistency between his behavior and Frank's may have been an issue. Frank had been a CEO who was more involved with his employees, but Jim didn't understand he needed to continue that behavior.

Leaders are expected to have high integrity, so inconsistency is a big red flag of trust. Consistency and predictability provide a feeling of safety for employees and greater trust in their leaders. Understandably, people are skeptical today; they need to be convinced that they can feel secure in their positions. They need to know that their leaders are capable of making the organization successful and that the roadmap their leaders offer will not lead the company astray.

In the book, *The Speed of Trust*, author Stephen M. R. Covey describes trust as confidence and the opposite of trust as suspicion. He says, "Distrust affects performance, instills less than optimal behaviors, and separates employees from management. Workers can only trust you as much as you trust them. With all that you have to do, why focus on nourishing trust? The answer is, can you afford not to?"

Trust is perhaps the most important ingredient in creating a harmonious organization focused on success and high octane performance. You probably have a strategy in place to gain the trust of your clients, your lenders, and your vendors, so why not have one for your employees and organization?

If You Want Employees to Trust You, Trust Them

You practice trust all the time, even when you don't feel it. Have you ever had to slide into the passenger seat and allow your inexperienced teenager to drive? It's pretty scary. I've done it twice, so I know. Handing over the steering wheel is unnerving, as is entrusting others to do the work you could do easily without them.

As a leader, you have to trust others *before* they have proven they can be trusted. It's difficult, isn't it? This is especially trying for new managers. When called upon to do this, you might worry that your employees aren't capable of doing as good a job as you could do. I had the same fears with my corporate team members. Knowing that my name was to be associated with the results of others kept me awake at night. Like most Renegade Leaders, letting go is hardly an easy task.

One Renegade Leader explained the struggle of delegation this way: "It would take me a half hour to explain how to do it when I could just get it done and know I can do it faster and more effectively. It's hard to delegate. Yet, I see the need to grow my people. In the end, I'm responsible for the outcome … even if they screw it up."

Yes, trust is risky; you become vulnerable when you're responsible for tasks completed by others. But remember that you got to be the leader you are because someone had faith in your ability to learn and grow, so you simply must have faith in others to do the same. One of the top employee engagement drivers is that opportunity to learn and grow. We can't grow unless we take the risk, even if it means failing forward.

When employees feel trusted, they do their best. When you say, "I'm going to see if you can handle this project," the fear of failure often sets in, which can lead to underperformance. Imagine teaching your child to drive and saying, "I'll try out your driving for a quick spin around the block, but if it doesn't work out, you'll never drive again."

You might laugh, but as leaders, we do this all the time. Have you ever delegated a project only to "hover," checking in over and over to make sure it's done correctly? Have you ever assigned a task, then given step-by-step directions to make sure it's done "your way"? Today's employees want to put their own colors on the canvas. Sometimes, they even like to paint outside the lines. If you let them, they may paint a better picture than you anticipated. The key is to share the paintbrushes.

Leaders who trust are open to hearing alternative opinions and are willing to let others influence decisions. They share information and resources, and they willingly delegate to both those who are eager and those who are too frightened to take on new responsibilities.

Building a Culture of High Trust

Have you ever heard the saying, "Employees join organizations but leave their managers"? This is frequently because their managers didn't trust them or were not trust-*worthy*. After spending more than 20 years working with leaders, I have heard all sorts of stories that spur distrust within organizations: employees who are reprimanded at reviews for behaviors that took place six months ago and were not addressed at that time; employees whose feedback is later used against them; ideas that are stolen by higher level managers, leaving the originator uncredited; managers who try to function on limited information due to the "information hoarding" of their superiors; and the traditional influx of gossip and interpersonal concerns that feed the virus even more.

In contrast, according to the Great Workplace Institute which rates the 100 Best Places to Work annually, leaders who trust their employees create great workplaces. My team has delivered the Great Workplace training program numerous times for our clients, sharing the characteristics of trustworthy managers, which include integrity, reliability, caring, openness, competence, loyalty, and fairness.

In order to become a trustworthy manager, you must be a fair leader, but understand what that means. Each employee is unique, and being fair doesn't always mean treating everyone equally. This is because the roles and responsibilities for one might not be appropriate for another in the same position. Therefore, you become a fair leader by listening to all viewpoints and giving everyone an equal chance to learn and grow.

Be open to trusting others and open to receiving feedback from them as well. If you assign a task, allow that individual to complete it to the best of his/her ability, allowing some wiggle room for creativity. Be clear about what you need, and come to an agreement about deadlines. The book, *Who Will Do What By When? How to Improve Performance, Accountability and Trust with Integrity* by Tom Hanson and Birgit Zacher Hanson, offers great examples of accountability conversations.

Can your teams rely on you? It's hard to trust others to do the work if you are unreliable yourself, if you make excuses, or if you play it safe versus playing to win.

One way to build a culture of trust is to do what you say you're going to do or what is needed by the time it's needed. Then, when you ask an employee for a report by Wednesday at 2:00, he/she will be more likely to deliver on time as well. First, however, ask if the delivery time you have requested is an achievable goal. Then, if you're asked to provide information to an employee, don't let your commitment slide because it isn't your priority. Reliability and trust are two-way streets.

Save the high cost of turnover, and build a high performing, cohesive, and creative team by investing in trust.

FORWARD ACTIONS
Nourishing Trust: Build from the Ground Up

1. Make a commitment to yourself and your team to be credible and authentic. Become the leader you were meant to be, not a copy of somebody else.

2. Be reliable and of high integrity. Never make an agreement that you don't fully intend to keep, no matter how small. If you ever fall short of meeting a deadline or agreement, apologize immediately to everyone involved.

3. Be clear about everyone's roles and responsibilities. Stay fair without favoritism. Never dismiss one person while engaging others.

4. Notice how you react to changes. Unpredictability in behavior feeds distrust. If you blow up or appear unable to handle difficulties calmly, staff members will become trained to hide problems until they escalate. Their fears may keep them frozen in place, not knowing the right action to take, but unwilling to risk dealing with your anger and judgment.

5. Be committed to your core values and the principles and values of your organization. "Walk the talk."

6. Have a trust conversation. Russell Hardin, author of Trust and Trustworthiness, notes the differences between trust, distrust and trustworthiness. Have a

team conversation, create three columns on a white board with "trust" at the top of one, "distrust" on another and "trustworthiness" on the third. Ask participants how they differentiate between the three and record their comments. Ask how these thee areas impact leadership and engage in a conversation about how they operate within your organization or department.

To put your results into overdrive, visit our "Nourish Trust" Accelerators at

www.TheRenegadeLeader.com

Chapter 4

INFLUENCE

Foster Leadership at All Levels: Embracing the Highest Standards

"Give people a place to make a difference and it's amazing what they can get done."—Dave Cote, CEO, Honeywell International

Jim invited himself to a staff meeting with Peggy and her team. He wanted to encourage them to be open and honest when preparing for the upcoming merger meeting. He had been practicing his inspired leadership and was getting results (in spite of a few confused faces along the way). His people really seemed to respond to his interest in them. He also learned more about their personal needs. He got them to talk about their career ideas and how he could better serve them as their leader, and he was surprised by how much he actually enjoyed listening to their responses. He finally got how relationship building could strengthen trust within the company.

Jim was also coming to terms with how often he and his management team stole the reins from others, not trusting them to take enough responsibility. "We have to enable our team to succeed within the organization. We have to allow them to have a say in decision-making and find their own voice," Jim told himself.

Even Julie benefitted from Jim's new insights. He asked his wife about the novel she was reading, what went on during her day, and where she thought they should go on vacation in the summer. He even promised that he would really be present during their vacation, not texting or checking his email every moment. The I.N.F.L.U.E.N.C.E. Framework outlined how he could get his business to run so productively that he wouldn't have to be there. Could he actually relax on vacation? It was an exciting prospect. Like other Renegade Leaders who make fast decisions, Jim was test driving what he had learned. He liked the experiment so far.

When Jim read about fostering leadership at all levels, his first response was, "What a relief it would be not to have to do it all!" His next thought was, "But what if they don't do it right?" There he was at trust again. Well, all he could do was give it a try. Although he was dead set on the merger, he understood that if he allowed others to come to the same conclusion that this was a great opportunity for their company, he would gain their buy-in and, more importantly, their commitment to make it succeed.

He wasn't sure how the meeting would go, but he assured himself that he could still pull rank at any time, if necessary.

The team trailed in, and as creatures of habit, they all gravitated to their usual seats. Some had notepads with them, while others brought only their three o'clock coffee boost. Peggy had documents in her hand and looked like a pillar of preparedness or a lioness ready to protect her brood. Jim was not sure which.

Rather than go for his usual seat at the end, Jim chose this time to sit on the side of the table, leaving the end seat open. It seemed to confuse a few people because they could no longer sit in their usual seats. Peggy took up one end of the table, and that end seat, which was the last one left, was taken by a bewildered latecomer.

"Thank you for taking time out to meet with me," Jim began. "I know you and Peggy have been working this week to take a long look at the merger, and I'm excited to hear your feedback. The merger impacts every one of us, and I want to make sure it's the right decision for us as a company, as well as for our customers, before we make a final decision."

"We" was not usually in his vocabulary, and Jim found himself consciously having to search for the word from deep within him. He looked around the room for reactions to his new use of words. They were hardly accustomed to his openness, but no one was fidgeting or drinking coffee. All eyes were attentive.

Jim began by asking the team to agree on their guiding principles for the meeting. Again, there were baffled looks.

"Guiding principles," Jim explained, *"are shared agreements on what we want to get out of our time together, what we're here to do, and how we agree to be with one another throughout the meeting."*

Steve was the first to speak. "I'd like to leave the meeting with a clear understanding of why we're looking to merge in the first place. Is there a problem with our current company?" he asked. Jim nodded and wrote "Reason for Merger" on the whiteboard. Normally, he would have a team member be the scribe, but today, he decided he would do it and allow everyone else to sit at the table as "mini-CEOs."

Carla shifted in her seat and said, "I'd like for everyone around the table to talk. Often, just a few of us end up speaking." Jim smiled. Wasn't that always the case? He wrote, "Everyone shares."

"I keep thinking about our clients. What will they think? Will I lose any clients to the merger?" Kyle asked.

Eventually, they decided that every voice would be heard, all ideas would be respected and documented, every idea would be addressed or scheduled for a follow-up meeting, and there would be no whining or swearing. Yes, that had happened in past meetings—quite often, unfortunately. (Peggy privately hoped there would also be no crying.)

The rules, issues for discussion, and concerns were written in the corner of the whiteboard in the front of the room, and the meeting began. Two hours later, all of the pages on the flip chart were used, and the whiteboard was filled from end to end. Most everyone expressed the thoughts they had been harboring. At times, voices were raised as if stretching to be heard, but their tone was quickly quieted once they were assured they really had the floor. Many questions were raised, some of which Jim had not even considered. And most importantly, decisions were made—not on the merger itself, but on what areas still needed to be reviewed.

Small focus groups were established, actions of accountability were agreed upon, and another meeting was scheduled in two weeks. Everyone walked out of the meeting still engaged in conversation.

"It worked!" Jim exclaimed to himself once he was left alone in the conference room. He got them to open up about the merger, expressing concerns he hadn't even thought of. "I hope I built some trust with them by exposing my thinking process to them. With any luck, we'll all get on the same page," he thought. Everyone seemed to like being given the responsibility to look deeper at the merger and to share viewpoints and learning with the entire team, especially the opportunity to do so in small focus groups.

The Framework had stressed that the biggest way to solve any problem was to ask others to join in determining the solution. Using the concept of successful masterminds, the collective intelligence of many far out-values the competence of one. "I think if they really look at this from all angles, they will see what a good opportunity it is," Jim thought. He left the conference room with a sense of hope and excitement that he could create the powerful organization he had always dreamed of.

Share the Front Seat

When you were a child, did you ever want to sit in the front seat with your parent? Did you ever "call" it, only to have an older sibling take it anyway? Jim had too often played the role of that older sibling, never letting his employees ride in the front seat. With the meeting, he broke that cycle, allowing everyone to see the whole picture.

It can be scary on dark, rainy nights when you drive alone. When the journey is long, it's better to have a few passengers on board, and it becomes a more interesting trip when you share leadership. Conversation flows, shortcuts can be discovered, and sharing the heavy role of leader gives you time to rest or plan for what lies ahead.

It's no surprise that the most driven, impassioned leaders hold the reins of leadership tightly in their fists. Trust concerns and worries about delays often keep them from sharing their responsibilities. But imagine what you would be capable of achieving if others stepped up to the highest level of leadership?

The bottom line is: Your role as a leader is to create more leaders. Fostering leadership now helps you pull together your team when you need them the most, such as when:

- You're trying to merge divisions or organizations together and are met with resistance.

- You're in a state of change, and some team members are inflexible.

- You're under pressure and need the collaboration and fine precision of your people to achieve your goals.

- Your responsibilities have grown, and you are wearing thin so that you just can't manage it all unless you delegate.

Yes, as a leader, your role is to be someone others follow naturally, but your secondary role is to inspire others to lead effectively as well. In fact, your job is not to just give them a seat up front but actually hand them the keys from time to time.

Leadership is Everybody's Business

We all lead from where we are; leadership is not a title, role, or compensation level. Excellent leadership involves the ability to think expansively, create a big vision, set actions in place, move toward that vision, and be self-accountable.

In traditional models, the leader was the expert, the brains of the operation, the go-to person, and the final decision-maker. Today's successful leaders realize they don't have to do it alone because they can create leaders at every level, and modern employees are yearning to take on more responsibility. They want to play a bigger game, use their brilliance, and contribute in the way that best serves their personal life purpose.

The good news is that as a leader, you don't have to come up with all the solutions—at least not if you foster leadership at all levels and inspire innovative thinking in your organization. Ask others to be part of putting the puzzle together when the pieces seem out of order. One of the top drivers of employee engagement is the ability to offer innovative ideas and provide input into the decisions made in their department. So, why hold back? It's a win win—you create greater employee engagement, increase the competency of your people, build trust, and gain more time for focusing your leadership on key projects.

Let's look at what has happened when leaders asked others to be creative. Boeing's popular 747 was created when the airplane maker organized a focus group of employees in a hangar with the assignment of answering, "What should we do next?"

FedEx established its overnight delivery service because one of its employees looked at banking and wire transfers and saw a way to develop systems that would allow for overnight delivery.

The ballpoint pen was perfected when an employee applied roll-on deodorant design in a writing pen. These were all tipping points for these companies, and they only happened because employees were heard and given the opportunity to share the role of leadership regardless of position.

Statistics have shown time and again that when employees step into leadership, services improve, productivity accelerates, and profits soar.

Jim's past frustration with his team meetings is not unusual. Employees often wait for a leader to give direction, to make decisions, and to correct problems. Instead, put leadership back into the hands of your staff around the table. Ask other leaders to step up. Invite them to look closely at an issue, running it through the microscope of your values and guiding principles, and returning with their verdict. Allow them to have a focus group, build a transformation team, or correct a problem by coming up with solutions that, again, meet your organizational requirements. They may come back with the same decision you would have made, or they may enlighten you with a business-changing tipping point. Either way, they will feel empowered, grow in leadership, become engaged by having a say in the company, and focus more on how they can improve the organization, its products, and its services.

FORWARD ACTIONS
Letting Others Feel the Power of the Drive

Here are some ways to hand over the keys:

1. Ask powerful questions. Others can't lead if you don't invite them in. Ask for their opinions, ideas, and concerns.

2. Create focus groups, although I prefer to call them "transformation teams." If you have an idea or problem you would like to resolve, put these transformation teams into the driver's seat, asking them to analyze and determine the next step to bring the idea to fruition or correct the situation.

3. Establish your decision-making values. In *Delivering Happiness*, Zappos CEO Tony Hsieh discusses the company's core values, upon which every decision is made: Values such as "Deliver Wow through service," "Do more with less," and "Create fun and little weirdness." Another organization uses three-legged stool guidelines for every decision, asking, "Does it benefit employees, the customer, and the organization?" If any of these fail, the decision is no. All three legs are needed for support; if one should weaken or break, the whole stool tumbles. When you establish shared decision-making criteria, everyone is able to make decisions using the same filter.

4. Work with your team to establish guiding principles of behavior. One client referred to this as "10 Golden

Rules." In order to adhere to your standards of excellence, what behaviors must be demonstrated daily? Remember that leadership is modeled. Employees don't know how to be leaders unless they are shown how to lead. Recognize those who follow your guiding principles, and you will soon have an entire team of leaders.

5. Train your people, and bring leadership to all levels. Recent studies show that leaders who have coaching skills create more than a 30 percent increase in performance than those leaders who lack that competency. Help your managers learn how to coach their teams more effectively as well.

6. Bring the topic of leadership into the room. Define what the word "leader" means within your organization. Talk about what attributes make great leadership and what behaviors model that effectively.

7. Set expectations for leadership. Expect others to be willing to be at bat now and then. Home runs are never hit from the bench, so get everyone into the game of leadership.

8. Have teams create a team competency development plan. Explain to team members that the team itself is also a leader, how well is it leading? Use an assessment; we use Team Performance to evaluate the collaboration, trust and capabilities of a working team. Your team can define what makes a great team

and evaluate its own team performance. Have them define the actions needed for their team to be a great leader and model for other teams.

To put your results into overdrive, visit our "Foster Leadership at All Levels" Accelerators at

www.TheRenegadeLeader.com

Chapter 5

INFLUENCE

Listen to Quiet or Unfamiliar Voices: Tuning into the Hum of Your Engine

"Find your voice and inspire others to find theirs."—Stephen R. Covey, *The 8th Habit*

The day after the staff meeting, Jim strolled down the hall to John's office. He noticed again that the executive offices were lined up on one side of the building, while sales, support, and middle management were on the other. "Have to do something about that," he said to himself.

John was chief financial officer for the company, a quiet guy who kept to himself. He was always polished in appearance, and Jim secretly admired how his office looked pristine despite the amount of paper he handled. John had great integrity; he owned the numbers in the company as if they were his own bank accounts, watching every penny and every decision with dedication. Jim sometimes suspected that John disagreed with him, but he never said so. Others might voice an opinion, but John always hung back and remained silent. Jim had come to the conclusion that John was capable of contributing much more and that he should be encouraged to do so.

John was hunched over his desk as usual, so preoccupied with his computer that he didn't see Jim at first.

"Have a moment?" Jim asked. John bolted upright, startled to discover that Jim was there. Jim sat down, noticing that John didn't have a meeting table in his office. Guests were forced to sit and face his large desk, so Jim made another mental note.

"I was thinking about the merger," Jim began.

"Did you get my reports? I think I gave you everything you were looking for," John quickly interjected.

"Yes, I got all that; thank you. I wanted to spend a few minutes with you to see what you really thought about it."

"The numbers all work, and we've secured the capital," John began before Jim cut him off.

"No, not just that. What do you really think? You've been my working partner for years, you make it all work together financially, and I trust all that. But what do you think about the merger and how it's going to impact you?" Jim asked.

John paused for a moment. "Well, Rumbletree has used outside people for their financials, so they should be okay with my doing the work for them now, bringing it back in-house. Their finances look solid, the best I can tell."

"But what about the effect on you, John? You were here late all week and probably take things home, too. How can you take on any more work? Let's get you some help."

"I'm confident I can do it," John quickly said, worried that Jim was questioning his ability.

John looked questioningly at Jim, trying to read him. Was he really offering help, or did he think John couldn't do the job by himself? Help would certainly be great. He could barely make it to his son's lacrosse games as it was.

"Yes, that might be a good idea, at least temporarily to get all the files in order, to merge the data, to merge accounts, and to make sure everything is accurate. What did you have in mind?"

Jim smiled. He knew John would need more than temporary help. He respected John's work and knew it was also time for him to delegate more so that he, too, could have time to develop bigger visions for the company.

"I think we need to hire a full-time staff person to make it easier on you and free you up to take on more important tasks. Come up with a job description, and let's get together with HR to get it approved. Once the merger takes place, we will be all set to go. Think you can have that done by Wednesday?"

John agreed, and Jim left with another smile of satisfaction on his face. John had spoken up and made a step toward expressing his opinion.

Are You Only Listening to the Squeaky Wheels?

Imagine for a moment that you're stopped at an intersection. If you were in our area in New Hampshire in recent years, you might have noticed an exotic red Ferrari rumored to be owned by rock star Steven Tyler of Aerosmith, who drives it in the state when he visits his father. Or your head might turn at the loud vibration of the altered muffler of an ambitious young driver. You might not even notice the older Honda on the other side of you.

The truth is that we tend to give attention to only what purposely attracts our attention. Just like Jim had failed for years to notice the missing meeting table in John's office or the fact that John was overworked, what might you be missing in your organization? Are you only listening to the people who are loud or who demand your attention?

When you're at your next team meeting, look around the table. Who are your idea generators? Your promoters? Your resisters? Are there one or two who are always perched on the edge of their seat, ready to share their ideas, advice, and expertise? Are there others who share their opinions with ease? Is there one who always disagrees or has to bring up the negative aspect of each opportunity, lengthening the time of the meeting, causing frustration, and (at times) saving you from a poor investment or decision? If so, great! It means that people are talking and contributing.

But what about the quiet ones who linger in the back? These are the team members who express an idea but fail to say it with conviction, so it remains unheard, like a slight breeze that just passes you by. Who in your group hardly contributes at all?

A great Renegade Leader finds a way to bring all of the voices into the room, helping team members with less confidence to have the courage to contribute. Encourage feedback from all team members, regardless of their position. Conversations rich with diversity are often the most creative, even when there are differences of opinion or people who are unsure of their suggestions. Questions can be just as important as solutions because they can guide you toward the best ideas. Open-ended, powerful questions, or points regarding the different facets of an idea can often lead to another conclusion. In fact, the biggest innovations come from people who ask "What if?"

Leaders who are determined to accelerate to their goal and quickly identify the next one might tune out team members who offer controversy or opinions without solid foundation. Many ideas are verbally shot down before they're ever explored. Other times, body language—a hand wave, crossed arms, or rolling eyes—indicates clear rejection. These gestures teach contributors to keep their thoughts under wraps.

Think of it as learned helplessness. If you can't contribute, you can't shine, use your brilliance, ask team members to explore why something might not work, or offer a business-changing idea. This is part of the disengagement factor in business today; employees reluctantly agree around the conference table and fail to be truly committed to the goal—your goal, your business objective.

Allow Everyone to Honk Their Horns

While true Renegade Leaders realize that great ideas don't just come from extroverts, how do you seek out feedback from quiet, reluctant people? Simply engage them in conversation.

If you believe you aren't getting honest feedback, ask your employees to provide their opinion anonymously through surveys or comment boxes. This eliminates the fear that the person making the comment or suggestion is going to be singled out or discriminated against.

Once you have received suggestions, you don't have to act on all of them or offer detailed comments about them, but the value of all contributions should be acknowledged. Let employees know what ideas are going to be accepted and the next action steps that will be taken. Ideally, give idea generators the opportunity to bring their ideas to maturation, perhaps by forming transformation teams to explore the concepts more deeply.

Are you worried that too much time will be wasted or that the ideas offered will be irrelevant to your organizational goals? Share your vision with your team, and ask them to add to the vision. When employees are part of developing the vision, they can easily identify the values and behaviors needed to support it. Creating a common lens through which everyone sees your vision also unifies your entire organization.

Listen With More Than Your Ears

When you receive ideas from your employees, don't just listen to the words. In coaching, we refer to this as "Level III listening." This means noticing the tone of voice, eye contact, and body language. Crossed arms could be a sign of disagreement, for example, or that the person is simply trying to warm his/her arms. If you aren't sure, ask. Otherwise, you'll never know.

I was recently asked to work with a team on goal-setting for the next quarter, but when I entered the meeting already in progress, I noticed that one of the participants at the end of the table had her arms crossed. I asked her if she had a concern from the prior meeting that she would like to discuss before we continued. She answered yes, and the team invited me to sit in while they concluded the conversation.

It's an acquired skill, but reading body language allows you to establish a better connection with your employees, especially the quiet ones who are less likely to verbalize their concerns. Upward eye movement, for instance, indicates that the individual is searching for the answer or is unsure. This gives you the opportunity to see if the person needs more details to make an informed decision.

If you're a parent, you might have read the book, *How to Talk so Kids will Listen and How to Listen so Kids will Talk* by Adele Faber and Elaine Mazlish, which teaches the art of paraphrasing and reframing to build effective communication. The same techniques work well in business communications. Let's say that a member of Peggy's sales team comments that the merger might mean less business for everyone. Peggy could reframe this concern as, "You're worried you won't have enough business to make your sales quota," which would bring the conversation back to the individual's fears, concerns, and personal impact. This allows the person to feel heard and also prevents the conversation from degenerating into blame or loss of focus.

So, when employees complain, listen to what lies below the surface. What is this person's true fear, belief, worry, or concern? What is this individual *not* saying while expressing frustration?

Get to Know Your Staff

Jim had paid enough attention to John to surmise that he was holding back his opinions. He also realized that John was probably putting in more hours than he should. The better you get to know your employees, the more easily you will be able to draw them out and find out what they need to be successful, as well as what they can contribute to create greater success for the entire company.

One day, a CEO called to tell me that she had just spent a lot of money on sales training, only to hear one of her top salespeople whining that she hated the training. This salesperson was certain the training wasn't going to work, and she didn't understand how the new sales language was going to help her. Another employee seemed very distracted in the meeting. The CEO had flown in for the training from across the country, so she was quite annoyed that her employees didn't seem to value being a part of the team or appreciate the investment made to help them develop their skills.

Knowing the CEO's staff, I quickly surmised what had happened. The individual who was frustrated with the training had a right to be. The CEO and I both knew that she was well known for her attention deficit disorder (ADD), and although she was a great salesperson, she had difficulty taking in so much information at once. Adults with ADD do better with step-by-step training that allows for interaction. Most of the training involved the facilitator delivering the curriculum instead of engaging with the participants.

The training could have easily been modified to engage this individual and others like her. As soon I explained this to the CEO, she understood as well and let her frustration with the salesperson go. She realized that all future trainings should involve interaction in order to provide optimal learning for her staff.

The distracted team member had previously shared her religious convictions with the CEO, and we knew she engaged in a moment of prayer every afternoon. Due to the tight training schedule, few breaks were available, lunch was brought in daily, and the employee was not given the opportunity to leave the room. Lacking support for her daily prayer break, she blamed the training and expressed her frustration. Of course, she had remained quiet, not expressing her needs to the trainer, and her manager had also failed to consider her unique situation and make modifications to allow her to leave the room for her break.

Paying attention to your team and encouraging their participation are all part of tuning into the hum of your organization's engine. Only then, will the sound be harmonious, with everyone working toward the same unified goal.

When you listen to the quiet voices, something magical happens. You begin to release the potential of your people. Stand back and watch what happens then.

FORWARD ACTIONS
Tuning into Your People

1. Ask, ask, and ask again until your employees understand that you really want their input: What do you think? If this was your project, what would you do? Where would you start? What would be the value to the company in doing this? How does this feel to you? How would this affect our people, our operation, our customers, and our bottom line?

2. Listen deeply for what is not said. Is this person very attached to the outcome? Is there emotion in this opinion?

3. Listen without reacting. When someone raises his/her voice, the person wants desperately to be heard. Honor that without rolling your eyes, slamming your fist down, acting like the idea is stupid, or proclaiming that you're going to do it your way anyway. (I have seen far too many Renegade Leaders exhibit these behaviors.) Instead, breathe! To be an inspired and inspiring leader, leave your judgment robe on the hook by the front door. Calmly take the idea, and, like a prism, hold it in the light, turning it all around to see every facet. Then, repeat number 1 again, asking powerful questions, and come to a joint conclusion. When you provide your team with all the information you have, more often than not, everyone will come to the same conclusion.

4. Listen for what's possible. So often we tune into what is not working, we focus on the problem and we tune into the emotion regarding a topic. When you hear a problem, ponder a solution, when you hear an innovative idea, make it bigger. Soon you will find your team members doing the same.

To put your results into overdrive, visit our "Listen to the Quiet Voices" Accelerators at

www.TheRenegadeLeader.com

Chapter 6

INFLUENCE

Unleash the Potential in Your People: Shifting into Overdrive

*"You say to yourself, if I could only unleash the power
of everybody in the organization, instead of just a few
people, what could we accomplish? We'd be a much better
company."* –Andy Pearson, former CEO, Tricon Global
Restaurants Inc. (KFC, Pizza Hut, and Taco Bell)

*Jim sat at his desk, flipping through the I.N.F.L.U.E.N.C.E.
Framework. Some of the pages were becoming worn, and one
was adorned with a circle coffee stain. He read the words
over and over again. He was intrigued but a bit remorseful
at the same time. While he recognized himself in the pages
and had been a competent leader, he realized his team needed*

him to be more than that. He had hung onto the old school way of leading by force, and he was coming to realize that he needed to loosen the reins. He finally understood that his need to be the go-to guy for final decisions and problem-solving was why he was so exhausted much of the time. He was primarily responsible for the success of the organization, but he was also primarily responsible for the fact that it hadn't yet fulfilled its full potential.

When Jim read about coaching skills, he saw himself as the "what not to do" leader. It was a rude awakening. He resonated with the directive to listen without reacting, and he knew he wasn't the only one in the office who had trouble controlling his reactions. In their team meetings, no one could finish a sentence without someone leaping in to add to the statement, argue against it, or take the lead on the idea. "I always thought everybody thinks and processes information in the same way. Clearly, I was wrong about that," Jim thought. "That certainly explains all the conflict we deal with in meetings."

A recent article by the Framework author referenced neuroscience and the idea of "leading with the brain in mind." She referenced the "neuroshifts" that today's leaders need to make in order to be successful. While Jim wasn't so sure of the science, he understood the concept and that everyone has a fight-or-flight instinct activated by the brain. "I never realized that how I speak to people can activate this part of the brain and send them into feelings of fear," he thought.

As he continued reading, he learned that one type of communication activated creativity and action, while negative communication could paralyze its recipient, disabling rational thinking processes and preventing them from being proactive or taking action. Jim had to admit that it made sense. "I can picture instances when people have become confused or unable to respond after I've raised my voice," he remembered. "I activated the fear part of their brain when my plan was to move them forward. Phew! Navigating these neuroshifts isn't going to be easy."

While he prided himself on his behavioral changes since reading the Framework, he knew he had more changes to make. Jim knew that stopping the habit of knee-jerk reactions and judgments wouldn't be easy either. "I have to learn to stop thinking of someone's ideas as right or wrong, good or bad, and I have to stop applying fault," he instructed himself. "The person simply is, and their actions simply are."

Jim was lost in thought once again when Rebecca, one of the company's top consultants, arrived at his door looking frazzled and short of breath. She didn't even ask if she could enter but just swooped right in like a little tornado. Rebecca wore many hats in the organization, but the one she took most to heart was customer service. When Jim looked up at her, he noticed that her reddened face nearly matched her vibrant ginger hair.

"It's happened again," she said, "and I can't stand it anymore. You've got to talk to Bob. Nelson Roberts is flipping out because of technical problems all day, and Bob told him he would get him the fix by 3:00. Now, it's nearly the end of the day, I can't reach Bob, and Nelson is getting madder by the minute. Can you find Bob and try to get this fixed?"

Jim cleared his throat and remembered the "listen without reacting" instruction in the Framework. He took a breath, and paused.

Nelson Roberts was a key contact at one of the company's largest customers. In the hope of providing the best service to the customer, McClarkson had assigned Bob Morrison as a dedicated technician for them. In the past, Jim would have hunted Bob down, picked up the phone with his adrenaline pumping and heart racing, and called Nelson to smooth things over. And he would have arrived home late for his own dinner as a result.

"Not today," Jim thought. "Today, I'm going to allow Rebecca to be the leader and try out this tennis ball stuff." Jim was referring to the "tennis ball management" he had read about. According to the Framework, tennis balls represent the problems, crises, and fires that others put into a leader's court to resolve. Using the coaching skill of powerful questions, Jim learned how to "tennis-ball" these issues back into the court of the person who brought them in.

Jim had always relished being the one who had all the answers, but those days were over. "This is an opportunity for me to tennis-ball the situation back to Rebecca and help her unleash her own power. She can solve this. I know she can," he thought before he spoke.

"So, what do you think should be done first?" Jim asked.

Rebecca looked puzzled. She wasn't expecting a question; she was expecting him to say he would take care of it.

"Well," she began, "we need to call Nelson and calm him down. Then, we need to hunt down Bob. I'm so angry with him doing this again! Where the heck is he?"

It took some restraint for Jim to sit quietly. He knew there wasn't going to be a "we" calling or calming anyone down.

"What will you tell Nelson?" he asked.

"First, we have to apologize that this happened again," Rebecca said. "Somehow Bob has to be more available if he's going to be the dedicated technician. Um... I know Nelson is looking for some data he needs for a report, so I'll ask him what information he needs. Maybe I can pull out just what he wants. I might even be able to access their files. I mean, he can't need all the data. Maybe he doesn't really need it tonight since it's the end of the day."

"That sounds like a good plan," Jim said. "I know you have excellent communication skills, and I'm confident you'll know exactly what to say to calm him down." He rose from his desk as if he were leaving the office.

"What about Bob?" Rebecca asked.

"You can talk to him tomorrow. He's probably handling another crisis somewhere. And if not, just remind him of our commitment to our customers."

Rebecca paused for a moment, hesitant to say anything more. Then, she quietly turned to call Nelson Roberts.

Jim reviewed the last five minutes in his mind. He had tennis-balled the crisis back to Rebecca and shared his confidence in her. She seemed to have a working plan, and he knew Nelson liked her. If she didn't panic, she could easily calm Nelson down. Jim also knew that she would feel great and empowered when she succeeded. He hoped she wouldn't yell at Bob about how he let her down. Instead, he hoped she would just remind Bob of his commitment to the customer.

Rebecca could handle this, but she would have handled it better with increased communication, coaching, and leadership skills. So, Jim made a note to look into bringing more training programs into the organization, probably after the merger, so that the skills learned would be universal. As he locked his office to leave for home, he could hear Rebecca on the phone with Nelson. "She sounds calm," he smiled to himself, "so everything must be going well." He turned and headed out of the building. "Tonight, I'll make it home in time for dinner."

Letting Others Go Full Throttle

Renegade Leaders like Jim are accelerators of their own destination. Like him, I'll bet you know how to work hard to stay on course while enjoying the speed, endurance, and adrenaline of the drive. But what if your management teams and employees want some of that adrenaline, too?

We've learned that a key factor of employee engagement is allowing others to grow and advance in their abilities, responsibilities, and careers. That can mean a new position in the company, an increase in salary, or additional responsibility. Most of today's companies are doing more with less, which means that raises are few, and opportunities for new positions are more competitive. Especially in that kind of environment, increased responsibility is still highly valued by employees.

Jim saw an opportunity to let one of his capable employees handle additional responsibility and showed confidence in her ability to do so. Take a moment to look at your job from the 30,000-foot level. Then, pull back even further, and look at the organization as a whole. Where are you empowering others to reach their highest potential? Who on your team would love to do more but needs an updated skill set to do so? Who would rise to the occasion if given the opportunity? When did you or your team last upgrade your skill sets or challenge yourselves to move into something unfamiliar?

Allow your people the freedom to fully engage their potential, to play a more active role, to shift into overdrive, and to experience their own power. Unlocking your employees' full potential not only provides improved business results, but it's a gift you give to your management teams and employees, as well as your customers, vendors, and lenders.

According to Andy Pearson, former CEO of Tricon Global Restaurants Inc., "Great leaders find a balance between getting results and how they get them. A lot of people make the mistake of thinking that getting results is all there is to the job. They go after results without building a team or without building an organization that has the capacity to change. Your real job is to get results and to do it in a way that makes your organization a great place to work—a place where people enjoy coming to work, instead of just taking orders and hitting this month's numbers."

Only through giving your employees permission to discover their own personal power and brilliance can you create the perfect workplace. Imagine leading so that others easily follow. Imagine having employees who are excited about arriving at work, with creative juices flowing. Imagine giving your customers a chance to tell you what they really need. Even lenders and vendors, if given a chance, can tell you what other industries are doing to stay on the leading edge and what you can do as well. When you let others go full throttle, you win, they win, everyone wins.

How Brilliant Are Your People? You May Never Know

Michael Dell began with custom computers at the University of Texas in the 1980s, John Nash had the support of Princeton University and MIT for his game theory, and, of course, Mark Zuckerberg brought us into social networking from Harvard in the 2000s. These colleges provided the inspiration for—and spirit of—innovation. What if they had told these students to stick to the usual curriculum and hadn't allowed them to explore their ideas?

Ken Steinberg, CEO of Cambridge Research and Development, says that it's important to get out of the way and allow your teams to face challenges. And he should know. He is a respected thought leader for many private and public corporations and an expert at providing insight and direction for entry into new markets and increased traction in existing ones. He is also a prolific problem-solver with a large portfolio of patents in numerous fields, including computer science, robotics, healthcare, and safety. He has managed numerous teams, breaking innovative ceilings with new strides in technology, and he mentors other thought leaders on how to do the same.

"The best problems in life are usually coupled with the biggest obstacles," he says. "It is one thing to fire up the team with a rousing call to action. It is quite another to convince them to put aside their doubt and find another way to win. Inspired leadership is the means by which you foster breakthrough moments. Inspiration is not framed in the context of what has been done, but what can be done." He suggests handing over the reins and allowing your team to regroup, recharge, and resolve what may appear to be an insurmountable problem. He believes that inspiration is most effective when solutions seem elusive and the team is living in the shadow of doubt. It is sometimes within these darkest areas that a brilliant thought is ignited.

Steinberg also stresses that a leader must intervene during a project or crisis only when necessary. "Overapplication is the quickest way to undermine effective leadership. Ill-timed and overapplied inspiration is transparent," he says. "While no one ever wants to see a team struggle, it is at these times when *your ability to inspire the best by saying the least about how they can achieve the most, will win the day.*"

One of the most courageous things you can do as a leader is encourage others to venture outside of their comfort zone and then, be willing to stand back and see what happens. I do this in my role as executive coach every day. Like a sports coach, know your team members well, including their personal capabilities, their challenges, and where they stop themselves due to fears or barriers.

Standing to the side might be the most difficult thing to do for a Renegade Leader who knows the answer, but giving the team the answer is like robbing from them. Plus, the answer they come up with as a team may be even richer than your own. You build greater results through collaboration.

Remember the I.N.F.L.U.E.N.C.E. Framework elements you've learned so far. First, create a culture of inspired leadership, nourish trust so that it's safe to express new ideas, foster leadership at all levels so that each employee has the organization's success in mind, listen to all ideas (including encouraging the voices of the quiet ones by offering them permission to share), and now: Unleash the brilliance in others.

When you unleash the full potential of your people, there's no telling how far they will go and, in turn, how far you and the company will go. Unless you do this, you have no idea how much power they have, and neither do they. So, help them discover who they really are, and allow them to live out their brilliance and succeed beyond their wildest dreams.

FORWARD ACTIONS
Giving Your Team a Chance to Show You What's Possible

1. Find out what your people need to be successful, and create a learning organization. Learning fosters pride and a sense of connection with the company. It also improves employee engagement and significantly reduces turnover. Companies we survey show vast needs in the area of effective communication, leadership development, time management, and keeping staff members accountable.

2. Allow your people to develop the skills they need to perform optimally, and challenge them to build skill sets that are beyond their current positions. Allowing employees to shadow jobs in other divisions or orienting them to the entire company helps them to see the big picture and understand the vast potential of the company. As staff members rise to the top, look to the horizon, and plan for succession. Groom

your ideal replacement as you continue to grow and advance yourself as well.

3. Create a mentoring culture where leaders support one another. New leaders who become managers often try to keep doing the activities that made them successful. The skills needed for new managers include planning, filling jobs, assigning work, motivating, coaching, and measuring the success of others. Reallocate their time from performing work to helping others perform effectively and delegating. Reallocating this time is difficult for many new leaders, as they have yet to learn the value of "management work" from the work that made them successful. Once they learn how to help others to be successful by managing their time, assignments, and resources, they create a successful culture of motivated performers.

4. Bring coaching competencies in-house. Coaching represents the most significant trend in leadership development within the last 25 years. You might wonder if coaching is any more effective than giving advice or direction, but coaching has been proven to decrease turnover by increasing loyalty and employee engagement. Managers who report to senior managers who are skilled in coaching outperform their peers by 27 percent. Employees who work for leaders who have been trained in coaching say they feel more valued, satisfied with their jobs, and, in turn, put greater effort into their work.

5. Know you have a potential to tap as well, so don't forget to continue your own personal growth and development. Rub elbows with other Renegade Leaders. In my company's Executive Briefing Symposiums and Renegade Leader Roundtable Mastermind sessions, leaders can share their visions with like-minded executives who are equally committed to success. You're busy, so let others bring you the information you need when you need it. The briefings include the latest in employee engagement studies, leadership strategies, neuroscience, and other topics that help you influence your results. (Information about these events is provided at the back of the book.)

6. Allow others to "fail forward." Taking risks is part of unleashing potential. Sometimes, the wrong choice is made, but without risk, companies cannot grow. Guide your people to take calculated risks. Again, if you are clear as a leader, they will make decisions based on the shared values and goals of the organization. When an error is made, acknowledge the person's willingness to move forward. After learning of a multimillion-dollar mistake, Google cofounder Larry Page once said, "We'll know better next time. But, oh, by the way, it's good you made this mistake. I'm glad, because we need to be the kind of company that is willing to make mistakes. Because if we are not making mistakes, then we're not taking risks. And if we're not taking risks, we won't get to the next level."

7. Create a Challenge Think Tank. Create a name for your conference room such as the Innovation Creation Workspace. Give your teams an opportunity to think bigger and to focus on improvements. Think Tank meetings allow participants to share and create, assign actions and accountability and, in the process, activate their full potential as a contributor.

To put your results into overdrive, visit our "Unleash Potential" Accelerators at

www.TheRenegadeLeader.com

Chapter 7

INFLU**E**NCE

Engage in Transparent Communication: Sharing the Authentic Spirit of Navigation

"Whatever your corporate mission, paint a clear and compelling picture that others can understand and embrace. State your mission in terms that appeal to your team's best instincts. Persuade and empower as if you are leading and mentoring volunteers." -Tony Dungy, The Mentor Leader

Jim sat in his office, reading portions of the I.N.F.L.U.E.N.C.E. Framework again. It talked about a report that the number one engagement driver for employees is knowing that senior management cares about them. The report emphasized greater

communication, especially transparent communication that shared the direction, goals, and status of the organization at any given time. "Another thing to do," he thought. "How can I possibly fit that amount of communication into my schedule? Every moment is taken up with running the company, working with the executive team, and setting the course for the future. Isn't that good enough?"

As CEO, there was a lot Jim had not shared with others. For a long time, he hadn't told anyone that he would like to acquire other companies and grow rapidly. The financial information was still held at the executive team level. "Doesn't this make sense?" he asked himself. "I don't want anyone to panic if money is tight, and I don't want them to become lax when money isn't tight." Yet, the Framework clearly outlined the benefits organizations gain when they share more information with their employees. It also apparently creates greater unity. He certainly wanted that, and he couldn't argue with the numbers that were presented.

Jim had also read that transparent communication increases productivity and profitability, and the news hardly surprised him. "It makes sense," he said to himself, "and building a sense of community won't be a bad thing. We'll become a national company with the merger, but I don't want to lose that family feeling Frank was able to build. We have our problems, but still, we've always been a family. I want to do the same when we grow, but the reality is that I can't spend a lot of time doing it."

Jim made a quick phone call to Roger, his technology manager, who answered the phone quickly. "Hi, Roger. I wanted to ask you about the merger. What kinds of new technology do you suggest for communicating with each other? We have email on the shared server, but that might not cut it. Do you know of something that can be more innovative, something that allows me to share what's going on without receiving tons of emails back or waiting for people to get around to reading their emails?"

Jim envisioned what his inbox might look like with the growing company. He hated email anyway. It was a necessary evil, but it kept him working 24/7 because he repeatedly gave in to the compulsion to check all of his devices whether or not the messages were urgent.

"Absolutely," Roger answered enthusiastically. He was happy to be asked for his opinion, and he definitely had some ideas. "We can use this time before the merger to venture into the new age," he said. "We can build our own in-house social networking platform. I can even create portals for sales, consulting, support, and management so that in addition to open communication, you can have work groups that communicate together, too. For you, I'd recommend video. Not only could I set you up with a video blog, but you could also use video to get messages to other executives, clients, and our vendors." Roger had never had the opportunity to demonstrate his expertise to Jim like this, so he was on a roll.

"I have read that clients who watch videos are 85% more likely to buy and that the open rate on video emails increases to 68%! The social networking platform and video will help us internally, but it will also better position our communication to our clients and potential clients," he continued.

"I like where he's going with this," Jim thought with a smile. "Using technology to increase client sales might also help with the internal costs of the social network development."

"Roger, this is great. Thank you. Please put together your recommendations." Jim said. "I just want something that I can do easily no matter where I am and that will take little time, and what you're outlining sounds exactly right."

"This could be exciting," Jim thought. The virtual communication systems that he had read about in the Framework made his company's technology sound ancient. Having a shared area for communication might be the solution he was looking for. It would help marry the companies together faster than the drip communication of an occasional in-house memo. It would give him an area to put the financial reports and sales forecasts so that all management would know how the company was performing at any given time.

Marketing had already been after him to do more social networking, and he needed innovations in order for the new company to turn heads in the industry. "I know everyone will be excited about it, and the investment sounds minimal in light of the return. This could save time, get information to each other faster, and even increase accountability because of the public exposure. I like it!" he thought.

Jim started thinking about how he had handled the news of the merger. If he had spoon fed the information to the management team, warming them up to the idea before springing it on them, there probably would have been less of a negative reaction. An in-house communication platform could have started a buzz of excitement.

He also realized that he didn't promote larger scale discussions or ask his management team about changes in benefits and the impact to their teams. Those decisions were made in the confines of his office. He now saw the value in opening up communication. "Full transparency is going to be a challenge, but I think I have to give it a try," he told himself.

The New "Communication Culture"

For Renegade Leaders like Jim—and possibly you—who have not been accustomed to practicing transparent communication, it can be a difficult transition. When confronted with the prospect, many executives respond with, "We already communicate through emails, phone calls, and written memos. I don't have time to do more." But organizations large and small are now making transparency a part of their culture.

When Adobe's financial team meets to discuss financial reports, their conversation is broadcast on the Internet for their interested employees to hear. eBay, the world's largest e-commerce organization, offers "Chats with the CEO" via webcast. Salesforce.com uses "Chatter," a social network platform that allows both colleagues and customers to share information and ideas. They use the same platform to allow their executive team to engage with their 5,000+ employees, offering a virtual real-time broadcast of their meetings.

The Great Places to Work Institute, which lists the Best 100 Companies each year in *Forbes* magazine, says that "two-way communication is arguably the most important dimension" of their model.

If you're still reluctant to take the time to create a communication portal like the one Jim is contemplating, think about your role as a leader. We've already talked about how to:

- Inspire employees to do what it takes to meet your strategic goals.

- Improve employee engagement by letting people know that their contribution is valued.

- Show employees that senior management and direct management cares about them.

- Offer training programs and other new skills that promote leadership throughout the organization.

- Keep employees informed of the vision for the organization, and allow them to have a voice in that vision, as well as some say in decisions.

A two-way transparent communication portal is a tool that can get you started toward achieving all of those goals, allowing everyone to help you navigate toward your vision. Remember that these are not just "nice to have" items; they are necessary staples for your organization to maximize its potential in productivity, profitability, and sustainability, and to minimize the costs of turnover by promoting employee loyalty.

As a busy Renegade Leader, your time is valuable, but so is your message. If you don't engage in open communication, neither will your staff. If you don't share the vision, others won't do the work needed to achieve it. Times are scary; if you are not communicating with them, your employees will become insecure, they will worry about their jobs, their performance will drop, and they will begin to look for jobs where they can feel confident about their future.

The Many Advantages of a Communication Portal

Most employees today are email and Internet-savvy, and many are avid social network junkies. So, make your communication part of their "addiction." Younger people especially love social networking because they want to feel connected to a community. This applies at work as well; they don't just want a job and a paycheck. A private communication portal creates exactly the sense of community that most employees want.

When you have a portal for transparent communication, you allow for a consistent message from the top down, and your employees understand why decisions are being made. Employees respond to transparency, whether it's good or bad. One of my CEO clients used her communication portal to inform employees as to why holiday bonuses were being waived. Financial constraints required that the company forego the bonuses in order to maintain health benefits for its employees. Shortly after posting her message about the bonuses, the CEO was surprised to receive a response from an entry-level employee, who had probably been looking forward to his annual bonus. He mentioned his respect for the organization, thanked the CEO for keeping everyone employed, and said he understood that the economy was preventing her from paying bonuses that particular year.

IBM has ThinkPlace, where employees can contribute ideas, and many other companies have created similar portals. This is especially important for organizations with many locations because it allows employees to feel that they're part of the corporate family, and it helps everyone to gain a deeper understanding of fellow departments.

Using technology for transparent communication is less costly than flying people in for meetings, is more personal than a memo, and allows everyone to feel connected each and every day. CEOs are starting online blogs, and their presence is felt throughout the organization. The message is consistent, and the language you use to describe your company and its future are the sound bites your employees will use when talking to potential customers, other employees, and the media.

The good news is that when employees understand the company, its history, its direction, and what makes it stand apart from the crowd, they perform better, become loyal to the company, and are able to easily distinguish themselves and their products or services from their competitors.

The bottom line is: If you want to get everyone on board, tell them where you're going. They need to know how to plan, pack and prepare for the journey.

What else can you do with a robust communication portal?

1. You can communicate the values of your organization by offering stories of customer experiences, rewards for community or industry involvement, and employee results that demonstrate those values. By posting your mission statement or values on your communication portal, it will remain top of mind for your staff.

2. You can recognize achievements (especially those that are in keeping with the values/mission statement published on your portal), a project done on time, an employee who went the extra mile, employment

anniversaries, customer testimonials, peer-to-peer recognitions, promotions, and more.

3. You can encourage certain behaviors, such as health and wellness habits, by providing information and resources or announcing a reduction in health care premiums. One team provided information, by department, on the cost of worker's compensation due to employee safety incidents. After becoming aware of these costs, the company's managers took action to educate their employees about safety procedures and incident reporting. Everyone set the goal to reduce or eliminate these costs to the tune of one department eliminating $175,000 from their budget, freeing up the funds for other projects.

4. You can build stronger teams by allowing members to have their own portal of communication for private discussions about projects, goals, and objectives.

5. You can conduct focus/transformation groups. Most people tend to believe in focus groups with skinny 15-minute (or less) meetings, but even these meetings can be eliminated or reduced when communication is shared through technology. The portal allows these groups to be accountable for their incentives, report actions, and request the resources they need to be successful.

6. You can use surveys to find out what your employees think about a particular idea or issue. The technology compiles the data for you.

7. Training and development is another potential aspect of your communication portal. My company has developed many Internet-based workshops for our clients that are easily portable into an organization's communication center.

8. Management teams can use these communication tools as well. One client refers to this part of the portal as the "Executive Circle," while another calls it the "Leaders of the Pack." It gives executive and leadership teams a place to share insights, ideas, and decisions about matters like employee benefits, mergers, acquisitions, and financial forecasts. It is also a place to review sales numbers and costs across all locations. When you add that competitive edge to the mix, everyone becomes fiscally responsible in driving results for the organization. After all, no one wants to be the high cost center or poor sales performer.

Transparent Two-Way Communication in the Real World

Tom Boucher, the CEO and Owner of Great NH Restaurants, adopted a transparent communication portal for his company, although he admits that he was apprehensive at first. "As an employee growing up in our company, I had always wanted access to more information," he says. "With our continued growth, it was more difficult for me to spend time with each location, yet I wanted to feel the pulse of the organization and to connect all seven of our locations into a unified company. It ended up being one of the best things we've ever done."

The company used its subsidiary marketing and branding company, The Scribbitt, to establish portals for its executive team and management for each restaurant, as well as open forums for employees to discuss a variety of issues. "Now, I can communicate directly with every employee, we can quickly take a poll, communicate financials, implement and process menu changes, and gain valuable front line employee feedback. Each employee has a personal page to post pictures, and interpersonal relationships are strengthened," Boucher says.

The company has experienced success despite the down economy, and revenues have grown at a rate that has allowed the organization to recently start another restaurant concept. "My dream of creating a unified company of shared values was achieved," Boucher says, "with open dialogue between employees, managers, and owners. I encourage other companies to do the same."

FORWARD ACTIONS
Establishing Your Own Communication Portal

1. Assess your current means of communication. Is it effective? Does it provide timely information? Are all departments aware of each other's goals, and are the overall goals of your organization discussed frequently? What is missing?

2. Ask your teams to design an effective system for transparent communication. What do they want to hear about? What are the most important topics? How can the system give voice to employees? How will the executive team share information?

3. Decide on a platform that is secure and easy for all personnel to use. Look into both in-house and web-based platforms.

4. Determine what discussion rooms or areas you would like to have on your portal and what type of information would be best offered in each. Will there be a human resources area for benefits? A CEO newsletter? An operations or safety portal? What about "In the News," "What we are doing in the community," or a "Shout Out" area for recognizing achievements?

5. Once you have the basic structure set up, consider using an assessment service to provide polls to quickly collect data from your employees.

6. Give a face to your communications through videos, which are fast, effective, and preferred by all types of learners.

7. Decide on the frequency of updates from executives. Old blog posts quickly become stale. Then, once a number is determined, keep your promise, posting as often as you have decided.

8. Develop an implementation rollout plan. One plan that has been used successfully is to begin with the executive team allowing key pages to be populated, followed by managers, and, finally, all employees.

9. Consider allowing employees to have their own pages where they can post information, allowing them to get to know one another better. What else can be added that will build a family-like atmosphere, even if your locations are continents apart?

10. Develop a "how to" guide to educate users on how to post, your posting protocol, on how the site will be monitored, and on what types of posts go where.

11. Launch the site by scheduling site enrollment days. Local managers can inspire enrollments by making access something valuable and desired.

12. Start to connect, engage, and weave unity throughout your organization, truly sharing the spirit of navigation toward your goals with authenticity and transparency.

13. Consider using video. The three most common learning styles are visual, auditory, and kinesthetic. Video optimizes that your message will be heard, understood and acted upon. Watching one minute of video is the equivalent of reading 1.8 million words! (Forrester Research).

14. Use communication to create the sound bites you would want your employees to use when describing your company, its direction and what differentiates you from your competitors. Repeating the same words instills the message that then becomes repeatable.

To put your results into overdrive, visit our "Engage in Transparent Communication" Accelerators at

www.TheRenegadeLeader.com

Chapter 8

INFLUENCE

Notice and Recognize Achievements: Celebrating the Mile Markers along the Way

"When employees feel well treated and taken care of, they try to add value and grow the business."—
Gamal Aziz, president and COO, MGM Grand

Toward the end of a particularly busy day, Jim's phone rang. It was Frank. "Jim, I just wanted to tell you that I'm really pleased with the way you've handled the company since I left. You've done a terrific job."

"Thanks so much, Frank," Jim replied. "I really appreciate your taking the time to call me and say that." Jim stood up and stepped outside of his office, watching his staff go about their daily business. Frank's call meant a lot to Jim, and he felt great as a result. When was the last time he did the same for his employees? He hadn't even mentioned to John how he appreciated the added work he had done to review the finances for the merger, and he had not thanked Peggy for her efforts in trying to maintain the morale of her sales team during this challenging time.

"Frank would have spent the time to do that. Of course, we were smaller then, and everything is so much busier now," Jim thought as he ran his hand through his hair.

Clearly, recognition wasn't just about reward systems and bonuses. Considering the boost that Frank's call gave him, Jim knew that his people needed a more personal touch. He started to write an email to John but soon decided to do something grander. He remembered when his consulting manager, Paul, shared correspondence that Zappos CEO Tony Hsieh had posted on Twitter. It was a letter to his company about Amazon's acquisition of Zappos.

Jim opened a file on his computer and began to write a similar letter to the entire company. He started by thanking them for their efforts, explaining that if it weren't for them, the company would not even be in a position to consider growing. He mentioned the glitches that they had experienced over the past year, which had caused some panicked customers, and he recognized his staff for bringing calm to the chaos. He cited his commitment to bringing new trainings in-house so that everyone could continue to grow and develop professionally, and he promised a new way to communicate that would reduce their time on email and bring the organization closer together.

He publicly thanked John, Peggy, Paul, and several other key employees for their dedication, and he expressed his confidence and trust in all of them. Finally, he told his staff how much he personally appreciated their efforts on the company's behalf and that he was proud and honored to work with each of them. He clicked "Send" and sat back with a smile on his face. It felt good to give back the great feeling he had received from Frank.

You Can't Afford to Ignore Performance

When we talk to leaders about recognition, many say, "We already have a program," while others roll their eyes. They feel their employees should be grateful to have a job and not look for more "pat, pat" on the back like the loving dog who demands constant attention.

How do you feel about giving and receiving recognition? Jim knew he valued the work of his people, but he knew he didn't always spend time acknowledging them. He also sometimes resented the notion that he was supposed to stroke the egos of adults. Nevertheless, when Frank called to acknowledge what Jim had accomplished, Jim couldn't deny that it mattered to him, and he realized that his employees must feel the same in that position.

When you ignore performance, your employees feel unappreciated, and that feeling leads to low morale and high turnover. Remember: It's easy to find people doing something wrong, and while it's important to correct mistakes, it's equally important to take the time to find people doing something right. Then, make sure they know you noticed.

In the book, *The Ultimate Question: Driving Good Profits and True Growth,* author Fred Reichheld suggests asking your customers if they would refer others to your company based on their experiences. Smart companies also ask the same question of their employees. Like most managers, you probably have a system for rating performance and offering raises or promotions, as applicable. But in most companies, this system operates once or twice a year at most. What happens in between?

The Las Vegas MGM Grand measures employee engagement annually. As a result, they report that 92 percent of their 10,000 employees said they would recommend MGM Grand as a great place to work. Eighty-nine percent said their work had special meaning and was not just a job, while 89 percent also said they planned to work there until they retired, and 90 percent said they experienced respect and dignity, a sense of equity and fairness, and satisfaction with both their jobs and the work environment. It can't be denied: When people feel valued, their loyalty increases.

What Types of Rewards Work?

When companies decide to acknowledge their employees, they often miss important opportunities. For example, much has been written about celebrating wins, but what about the mile markers along the way? The downside of celebrating only the wins is that progress is not recognized, and there is no evaluation of what it took to get to that win. Without recognizing the small wins, the big win has a short-term focus. Often, another goal is then quickly assigned, and great performance is forgotten.

What if you can't give a financial reward? Financial initiatives are fine, but what happens when they come to an end? While you can change behaviors based upon a prize, these behaviors are often short-lived. A moment of verbal recognition during day-to-day management or public recognition can be far more beneficial.

Let's look at the impact of real recognition. When Great NH Restaurants implemented its in-house social network, this platform was also used to make announcements and recognize high-performing individuals. Manager Mark Ferreira was one of the people recognized on the portal, prompting him to send a note to the CEO accrediting his success to the company's continued investment in its people. "I hold this to be the accomplishment I am most proud of in my life to date," he said. "The reason I care about our company is because aside from the work that I put in, this company has compensated me generously. It is not the material things or the money I am speaking of when I say 'compensate.' It is the knowledge I've gained that has been the greatest gift T-Bones has given me."

In Mark's case, he was motivated by being a part of a company that values its employees. The key to the recognition process, however, is to know what specific type of recognition is favored by *your* employees.

In the book, *Not Everyone Gets a Trophy,* author Bruce Tulgan talks about how to recognize Generation Y employees, for example, who were born between 1978 and 1990. Tulgan calls this group the highest maintenance workforce in history, but he says that they also have the potential to be the highest performing if given the right motivation.

Many of the companies I have worked with have struggled with managing this particular sector of employees, a group that demands strong leadership and clear rules so that they can do their work and know, like playing a video game, how to get to "the next level." The most socialized generation, they require connection, community, and knowing that they're a part of something bigger than themselves.

Rewards that this generation appreciates include flexibility in work schedule, technology use privileges, performance-based compensation, access to decision-makers, and opportunities for creative expression. They are also concerned with social responsibility—another driver for employee engagement—so it is important to them that their company is environmentally conscious. This "package" is far more motivating than a one-time prize or reward.

Recognition in the Real World

Marviel Martinez is regional West Coast vice president of Dick's Sporting Goods. He has more than 20 years of experience in retail and management. While on a cross country plane ride, I met Marv, and we talked for hours about leadership. "Noticing and recognizing achievement is very important to me because our associates work hard, they have tremendous pride in what they do, and they put a lot of efforts into their work. Our associates 'live the brand' each day," he told me.

Marv has realized how important it is that someone at his level takes the time to recognize employee efforts and achievements. He has noticed that people give a little more effort and put more passion behind their performance when they know they're likely to be recognized for what they've accomplished. He even developed a system to make sure that he maintains his commitment to recognition. He tours different regional locations with ten pennies in his right pants pocket, and each time he recognizes someone within the store, he transfers one penny to his left pocket. He never leaves a store until all ten pennies have been moved into the left pocket.

Marv also learned early that public recognition can work toward building overall team morale while driving competitive juices. "Praise in public, and coach in private," he says. He hosts weekly conference calls with the company's store managers, and at the beginning of each meeting, he mentions the top sales and profit performers for the week.

"Recognition, when done correctly, can be the deciding factor between flawless execution and poor execution," he says. "I have a quote that I live and lead by: 'Work hard, treat people well, and listen to what people are telling you.' The 'treat people well' part is about treating people fair, with respect and recognizing their achievements."

Marv activates the I.N.F.L.U.E.N.C.E. Framework, and that's why he gets results. He has discovered that verbal praise, presence, and authenticity require no investment other than a moment of time.

FORWARD ACTIONS
Shining It Up from Time to Time

1. If you can't be accessible via an open door policy, use your communication portal as a means for recognition. Encourage employees to recognize one another. Acknowledge "above and beyond" behavior. Use storytelling to showcase top performances by relating to everyone what the employee did, what results occurred, and why this ties into the shared

values and vision of the organization. (We even showcase Renegade Leaders in our "Who's been spotted" segment of our newsletter. Perhaps we will showcase you!)

2. Create performance-based rewards. Determine what rewards matter most to your employees, and establish a standard for recognizing high performance with financial benefits, upgraded title, schedule flexibility, and other rewards.

3. Practice day-to-day recognition, and train your management teams to do the same. Model this recognition for your managers, and put ten pennies in your pocket to remind yourself to do so.

4. Know what praise and appreciation works for the person you are acknowledging, and customize your efforts.

5. Write a note to the individual or their family, indicating their value to the company.

6. Take a staff member out to lunch; one-on-one time is highly valued if you can spare it.

7. Use your company newsletter or communication portal to give credit where it is due.

8. Share recognition with your customers on company wins, as well as client successes (with their permission, of course).

9. Be creative; rewards don't have to cause a strain on your finances. Build a revenue thermometer to help teams achieve a goal. Keep it visual, and make it fun. Use small gifts to show your appreciation—www. baudville.com has tons of offerings from thumbs-up tokens to other items. Use everyday items to show value: a stick of gum to say someone is "sticking with the project," glue for "holding the team together," and so on. Don't laugh! These little tokens, which seem small, can have big value.

10. Schedule appreciation for others into your day, making it part of your routine. Showing gratitude actually reduces your blood pressure, causes a great release of serotonin for both you and the recipient, and creates a feel-good culture.

To put your results into overdrive, visit our "Notice and Recognize Achievements" Accelerators at

www.TheRenegadeLeader.com

Chapter 9

INFLUENCE

Create a Culture of Collaboration: Teaming up for Championship Performance

"In Africa there is a concept known as Ubuntu—the profound sense that we are human only through the humanity of others, that if we are to accomplish anything in this world, it will be in equal measure due to the work and achievement of others."—Nelson Mandela

Jim was happy to hear voices already in the conference room as he walked down the hall. It was time for the follow-up meeting about the merger to discuss the pros and cons everyone had pinpointed, and the sales team's banter told him they were ready.

He was slightly concerned, though. He hoped the meeting wouldn't be a "whine and cheese" party, where he had to stand at bat and try to shield himself from every negative perspective they could think of throwing at him.

No, he was determined to have a good meeting. This time, he wouldn't attract the attention of a hallway bystander who might peer into his fishbowl of a conference room. His voice would not be raised, and his hands would remain at his sides rather than flailing in the air.

He greeted Peggy, who looked a little tense, her lips pressed together. Her teammates' eyes darted toward one another, and several people sat with their backs straight, as if ready to begin but apprehensive about it.

"So, Jim, we had our meeting and prepared a list of pros and cons about the merger," Peggy began. "Meredith also did some online research to help us look at Rumbletree."

"Great," Jim said. "I assure you that John has turned over every financial stone, and Legal has put together a rock solid agreement. It will be an organizational decision if we decide to move forward or not. I know that a vast number of mergers don't succeed because they neglect the human dimensions. That's why I want to hear your thoughts."

Jim paused, looking around to see if Peggy's team was becoming defensive. He scanned the room, and all seemed to be receptive. "Today, let's talk about the impact on sales, your department, your customers, and you personally. I want to hear your ideas."

Peggy looked around to see if someone was willing to start. Feeling their hesitancy, she spoke up. "We did find that Rumbletree has a good history," she said. "There were a number of positive client testimonials on the web. They have a Facebook fan page, too. From John's research, they appear to be financially stable."

Sue, crowned the office note-taker some time ago, got up and wrote "financially stable, positive customer feedback" on the whiteboard under the "Pros" column.

"But how will we divide up sales opportunities?" Mark asked. "Will they be in our territory? It's hard enough to close sales now with the few prospects we have."

Sue wrote "sales competition" on the opposite side in the "Cons" column.

"Let's just get all of the ideas down, and then, we'll address each one," Jim suggested, hoping the team would not focus on the negative too quickly.

"Their in-house technology is better than ours," Peggy added. "John said they have a great customer relationship management system and a database of leads."

Sue wrote "advanced technology" on the Pros side.

"They also have an 800 number," Meredith said, "so customers can call in and log their problems or access frequently asked questions to figure it out for themselves. That might save us some support time."

Sue wrote "customer service" on the Pros side.

"I'm not sure I like their reputation," Mary said. "I've competed against them before. Their sales rep was sneaky; she was all over the company, going from the CEO to purchasing. She also took the CEO out to meet with other executives and got her other clients to call him. No wonder I lost the deal."

"You lost the deal, Mary, because they used relationship building," Peggy chimed in. "We competed on product, and they competed on relationship building, which is something we could all learn to do better."

"Relationship building" was added to Pros.

The meeting went on for just over two hours, which was a bit longer than planned. Jim watched patiently as the team addressed organizational attributes, circling back to technology, branding, logos, what to tell customers, and how to merge products and services.

He knew it was going to take a little while to get to the key question. What was bothering them most? This was what the Framework referred to as "the unasked question." Finally, it came from Sue, as she faced the whiteboard.

"Are there any duplicate positions?" she asked. "Will you be keeping all of us?"

Jim looked at the faces around the room. Some looked at the floor, hoping perhaps not to be seen should staff need to be reduced. Others looked up anxiously.

"We already looked at that," Jim said. "Great question, Sue, and thank you for having the courage to ask it. I'm sorry that I haven't been more forthcoming with that information, and I plan to

be more transparent in the future—I promise. We are not planning to downsize. We do have some overlap in administration, but we can use that as an opportunity to off-load some of the customer communications to them, as I'm sure they'll have questions, too. Plus, with the merger of products and services, I suspect we're going to get more business and could use the additional support to handle the contracts and new customer orientations."

"What about management?" Mary asked. "They have a sales manager, too. Will we still report to Peggy?"

Now, it was time for Peggy to look directly at Jim.

"Yes," Jim said, "we think sales should be centralized from here. Their sales manager has agreed to step into a technology director role to oversee how the merger of technologies is going to mesh into sales and how to best present it to customers. His wife is expecting their first baby, and he seemed relieved that he wouldn't have to be available to the entire sales team. He'll work behind the scenes and still have great impact on sales. I talked to him late yesterday, and he told me his team is really supportive about it. The office was giving him a baby shower at the time."

Peggy's team looked at each other around the table. A baby shower? Jim rarely allowed more than a birthday cake to come into the office; maybe merging with the new company would mean some added fun.

"Peggy will manage the merged sales team, and I'm sure she will be happy to hear that we'll give her the sales admin person from their group to support her as well," Jim added.

"So, let's look at the board," Jim stated confidently, knowing that the Pros well exceeded the Cons at that point. He was proud

of the team; they had dug deep, determining what concerns their customers might have, how to address them, and how the new merger would better position them with prospects and eliminate some of their smaller competitors. Customers would be better served, technology would be enhanced, and everyone would keep their jobs. Still a bit unsure, the team agreed that the merger made sense. Great! Now, everyone was in agreement. The merger would be supported.

When the meeting was over, Jim took stock. It was clear to him that his lack of transparency had caused a lot of anxiety among his staff. If he had kept them informed of much of what he told them during this meeting, a lot of the negativity could have been avoided. He finally understood what a culture of collaboration truly meant and how each aspect of the I.N.F.L.U.E.N.C.E. Framework led to and enhanced the next, and he could clearly see the benefits of putting it into practice.

Collaboration is in our DNA

Renegade Leaders like Jim are horizon-gazers. They imagine the opportunities available to them, and it is their passion for the dream that spurs others to act. But leaders rarely do anything significant on their own. Effective leadership is about inclusion and getting championship work done in teams, so only by enlisting others in their vision can these leaders reach their destinations.

Ubuntu—the philosophy mentioned in Nelson Mandela's quote at the beginning of this chapter—values the success of a group above that of individual contribution. Ubuntu is the energy of the I.N.F.L.U.E.N.C.E. Framework.

In fact, we are actually "wired" to collaborate. Neuroscience helps us to understand human dynamics. When we collaborate with others, our brains light up with excitement, providing a scientific basis that working with others is preferable to working alone.

The next time you're around very young children, notice how they collaborate with great ease. Everyone gets a role in the imaginary play, all are enrolled into the projects that take place in the sandbox, and if someone is available, they are "in."

Not only does collaboration feel good (no matter how old we are), but it creates great workplaces and positive effects on the bottom line. This is why creating a culture of collaboration is a key component of the I.N.F.L.U.E.N.C.E. Framework.

The excitement of the shared journey fuels your organization with a vibration and a sensation that is palpable and uplifting. Imagine leading a team that embraces change and welcomes challenges. Picture working in an environment where success is contagious. You can build a company culture in which the positive energy can be felt all around, and your teams work together to share ideas and synergy, creating new solutions and new paths to reach successful outcomes together.

Laughter will fill the air, heads will be together in discussion, people will arrive at meetings on time, ready to share, and leave ready to take action. Phone calls will be answered quickly, customer service issues will be resolved, and absenteeism and turnover will be decreased. Employees will want their friends to work where they work and readily refer others. Proud of their company, employees will become the outreach face in the community, sharing news about your organization with others in the grocery line. This is where the magic happens, and it isn't a fairytale. Other companies have made this a reality.

REI, a company that sells backpacks and outdoor gear, has a mission to "inspire, educate, and outfit for a lifetime of outdoor adventure and stewardship." In their culture, employees are encouraged to dream up and coordinate activities that utilize their products.

Campbell's Soup's three stated values are "Character, Competence, and Teamwork." CEO Doug Conant says, "To win in the marketplace, we must win in the workplace," so every six weeks, he talks about these values in a meeting, where teams can creatively think of new ideas for products, services, or processes that optimize these values.

McKesson uses the acronym "I-Care: Integrity, Customer first, Accountability, Respect, and Excellence." Town hall meetings are held to discuss these values with employees and to gain feedback on how to make them alive in their day-to-day operations.

Share Your Vision

Your excitement about your vision will excite others, so begin by sharing it. Remember to connect the dotted lines so that your vision has a purpose that others can relate to. Why does the vision matter at all? How will it impact the work of each individual? Where does it fit in the commitment to your customers, your stakeholders, and your community?

Don't be afraid to express your passion and even your vulnerability if you're unsure how to make your vision a reality. President John F. Kennedy didn't know how to put a man on the moon, but he was committed to making it happen and got others to think about and create the possibility.

Why not paint your picture as big as it can be? Others might be able to define the possibilities. Put the putty of your vision into everyone's hands, and let them play with it for a while to see what they can create. Being a part of building the vision energizes the excitement to achieve it.

Just as children seem to know who will be good at doing what and quickly assign the right roles to individuals, identify the work to be done by all of your team players and decide who will do what and why. Do this as a collaborative effort as well, identifying what is needed and asking who is ready to step up to that responsibility. The people who move forward might surprise you. People take pride in tasks they have specifically chosen to perform, so involve your team players in creating the vision, as well as identifying the actions and timeline needed to get there. Ask what resources they need to be successful, and provide what is required along the way.

Collaboration moves along like a vibrant hum when the vision stays alive. If you want others to whistle while they work, keep the music playing. Keep people informed of the progress being made, or have your focus groups do so. Share the wins, challenges, and detours made as the project progresses, and reconstruct the journey around hazards and barriers that attempt to hinder your movement.

Then, don't forget to mark your successes with celebration. You did it together, so stand back and enjoy the view, asking others to see what you created. Get the word out: Use press releases for significant accomplishments, and inform your customers, lenders, and vendors.

Even the hardest tasks are easier to handle in collaboration. Now that your collaboration muscle is strengthened, focus on what's next. What else will make a difference? Where will you go from here? Use your shared values as a way of creating new ideas for your organization.

Collaboration begins with you. Know that you can't do it alone and that organizations that foster teamwork outperform those that operate in silos. Rediscover your playful side, engage others in the art of creativity, figure out how to keep the buzz alive, and make collaboration a core value in your organization.

FORWARD ACTIONS
Learning to collaborate toward a vision

1. Make your goal a destination, and share it vividly. Describe it using all of your senses, and keep it alive with a visual, compelling image.

2. Appeal to others to join you on the journey, allowing them to add their paint colors to the canvas. Talk about why this work, project, or destination matters and how it ties into the core values and commitments of the organization. Win over anyone who is reluctant by making the vision relevant to them and giving it personal meaning.

3. Track the mile markers along the way, and wave the flag to encourage movement. Stay agile enough to change direction or take a more scenic route when necessary.

4. Don't hog the shovel all by yourself; play nice in the sandbox. Ask others to take on tasks, to drive the project home, or to complete its roadmap. Develop task groups or focus groups, and make it part of your routine to talk about and create the future.

5. Spend some time at the destination. Too often, Renegade Leaders are so happy when a project or action is complete

that another is quickly assigned before there is time to relish the accomplishment. Take time to look at what you and your teams created, and take it in before the sandcastle disappears.

To put your results into overdrive, visit our "Culture of Collaboration" Accelerators at

www.TheRenegadeLeader.com

Chapter 10
INFLUENCE

Enjoy and Respect Diversity: Developing Cultural Intelligence

"As Americans, we live in an increasingly diverse population. At the most basic level, respecting diversity means recognizing the demographic reality that every leader is operating in an increasingly diverse and global marketplace where top talent comes in every gender, race, and nationality imaginable. At a deeper level, leadership is about empowering people within your organization to work toward a collective goal. In short, engaging diversity leads to organizational strength." –Kerry Ann Rockquemore, executive director for the National Center for Faculty Development & Diversity (www.FacultyDiversity.org)

"When people perform in roles in which they play to their strengths," Jim read in the I.N.F.L.U.E.N.C.E. Framework,

"studies show that performance and satisfaction increases, productivity improves, and they have a greater chance of achieving their full potential." The document went on to share how to discover the best in your people and how to value the differing life experiences, values, and rich cultural differences everyone brings to work each day.

The Framework promised the intangible benefits of productive teams, enlivened creativity, knowledge sharing, trust, and loyalty, as well as the measurable benefits of increased productivity, sales, profitability, and reduced costs, turnover, and complaints. "Well, I can't deny I want all that," Jim said under his breath.

He had always hired people based on their abilities. Sometimes, they lacked experience, but their optimism in learning the requirements of the job impressed him. He considered himself a good judge of character and prided himself on the managers he had hired. He also gave them some latitude to pick their candidates of choice, although he didn't always agree with their recommendations. He felt good about his team, but he had to admit that he hadn't thought about the need to educate his managers in cultural competence.

"Wow," Jim suddenly realized, "We do change our marketing depending on the demographics of those we're targeting. Doesn't it make sense to understand our own cultural differences better?"

He remembered how his team had expressed concerns about his youngest employees, Sheila and Ken. Both were in their twenties and were highly ambitious. They were happy to prove themselves within the organization, probably the most verbal of his staff members, and always willing to share an idea or two at the staff meetings. He had noticed some eye rolling from his older employees when Sheila or Ken made a point.

Then, it hit him. "The Millennium generation! The Framework said to educate managers on how to lead younger generations and to accept their self-knowing attitude as confidence instead of disrespect." Unlike previous generations, the Framework had said, the Millennium generation doesn't believe they need to climb a career ladder; they arrive ready to take on the upper rungs. If his management team grew to appreciate this aggressiveness and confidence, they could inspire their younger employees to achieve even more. When Jim thought about it, he recalled that his managers acted the same way with the intern last summer. They didn't value what this younger generation had to offer. "In order to respect diversity, we need to understand talent differences and why those differences exist," he thought.

Several managers also complained because Sheila and Ken didn't appear to be busy. Yet, when checked, their workload was always done. The secret was multitasking. Jim knew this because he had seen his daughter text, talk, and surf the web all at the same time, while also browsing a magazine! "Sheila and Ken will probably be the first ones to surf the company network and make friends with the merged company's employees," he chuckled to himself.

Jim actually admired their style. Like him, they had fire and independence in their bellies. They would stay where they were valued, where they continued to grow and learn, and where they were part of a community. If none of those criteria were met, they would go elsewhere. "Now, to get the other managers to understand that," he said out loud.

Then, he remembered Jose. A talented consultant, Jose often talked about his family and holidays. Others considered him to be less committed when he reached for his coat and was out the door before the clock struck five. Jim thought of Jose's devotion to his wife and children, the obligations he had to his extended family, and the joy and pride he exhibited when talking about his kids. Being home with his family was a key cultural value for Jose. Jim wanted to run an organization that supported the unique differences of each employee, yet built together the shared values that would get the work done and produce the highest results for the company and its customers. "I'll bet Julie wishes I would become more like Jose," Jim smiled.

He had to admit that enjoying and respecting diversity had been lacking on his radar. "If diversity awareness deals with creating a workplace where individuals understand and respect the differences in race, gender, religion, cultural values, and thinking styles, do we have this understanding and respect?" Jim shook his head and had to offer an honest no as his answer.

Perhaps a cultural assessment might be a good tool after the merger to understand the makeup of the culture and to identify its unique hum as an organization. He mentally added this item to his growing list of organizational improvements.

Learn to Leverage Diversity

Jim would benefit from looking at the New Jersey Institute for Technology as a model for his goal of respecting diversity. While it's a school rather than a company, many of the principles applied there would work in any organization. It has one of the most diverse student bodies in the country, so its Commuter

Assistance and Resource Services office works very hard to make sure that commuting students feel included in the college and able to sample all it has to offer. The school offers monthly celebratory events, including cultural heritage and cross-cultural forums. Students are valued for who they are, inspired to learn about other cultures, and appreciated for their brilliance and curiosity. Wouldn't every organization benefit if it did the same for its workers?

The world is truly flat; organizations today enjoy a workforce from multiple cultures, and teams often encompass not only the people down the hall but other employees across an ocean.

From what you've read so far, the I.N.F.L.U.E.N.C.E. Framework is a quilt of activities woven together with the common thread of building strong relationships. Bringing out the brilliance in others and creating a trusting environment where it is acceptable to be different, to have varied opinions, and to challenge group think are all key pillars of the Framework.

Appreciating the value in diversity is an important attribute in building the strongest of relationships. Know that your organization is made up of its own patchwork of multiple cultures, behaviors, and thinking patterns, creating its own vibrant rainbow, and learn how to leverage that culture. This is what makes an already successful Renegade Leader not only just more successful, but truly great.

How Does the Cultural Intelligence of Your Company Rate?

Defined as an individual's capacity to function, interact, and manage effectively in diverse settings and backgrounds, cultural intelligence is about understanding that a person's cultural identity has a great influence on how he or she thinks, makes decisions, behaves, defines situations, and determines success.

As the demographics of work populations change, it's important that leaders develop the cultural confidence and competence to successfully interact with others who are culturally different. You probably have a strategy plan for business results, but ignoring diversity is sure to slow you down.

Cultural differences are frequently ignored or given minor focus within organizations, which often leads to miscommunications, conflicts, and turnover due to frustrations, financial losses, and even missed opportunities. As a result, these differences can significantly impact performance. You want to be understood by others, and they want to be understood by you. Failure to recognize cultural disparities and their importance can block collaboration on shared goals, hinder accountability, and leave employees feeling misunderstood or unsupported, all of which creates roadblocks and potholes on your road to success.

Let's begin by understanding the definition of culture. The word is bandied about a lot these days, but what does it truly mean? "Culture" is a set of characteristics that distinguishes one group from another. Often thought of as ethnicity, culture also includes education, gender, industry, religion, organization, and function. While your culture is molded by your experience within your family of origin, your personality and behaviors continue to be shaped by those with whom you associate. A big influencer is your company's workplace culture.

Cross-cultural assignments, such as a multigenerational workforce, leadership teams during mergers and acquisitions, or leaders with clients in diverse markets, involve a higher degree of interpersonal and systemic complexity. As a leader, you simply cannot afford to deny the role culture plays in your organization.

The Value of Mentoring

Kerry Ann Rockquemore, executive director for the National Center for Faculty Development & Diversity, speaks worldwide on the important topic of diversity and why it is an essential component in today's business conversation. She says that investing in a broad range of professional development pays off for organizations. "The typical sink-or-swim culture is conducive to some people's growth, but not everyone benefits from this model. And in the long run, it can cost companies valuable employees," she says. She emphasizes that mentoring programs which provide both professional development and formal mentoring relationships have been shown to work very well. This is how people who may not automatically fit into the company culture find their way, gain the skills to thrive, and eventually become part of the fabric of the culture itself.

"Mentoring is too often seen as something that people can figure out themselves, and it's assumed that new employees will just find a mentor if they want such a relationship," Rockquemore says. "The problem is that the very people who would most likely benefit from mentoring relationships are the least likely to seek them out." When formal mentoring programs are available, there is a visible expectation that collaborative relationships are a normal part of how the organization operates and an accessible point of entry.

Respecting diversity in an organization is one of the most important strategies for building trust, inspiring employee loyalty, and creating an all-around better experience for everyone. This is because cultivating diversity allows you to make the most of your team's talent through encouraging creative and synergistic cooperation among team members. It also helps to build a level of appreciation for differences, which spills over into the way that your employees deal with clients and customers.

When we don't push ourselves to recognize our own unconscious biases (why we repeatedly trust, like, support, and lean on people who are just like us), we don't open ourselves up to the wide range of potential ideas, talents, and gifts of others.

Diversity is about creating a level playing field, a fairness of opportunity for all regardless of gender, age, religion, or sexual orientation. Respecting diversity goes even beyond that: valuing the opinions of others, their individualism, and their creativity.

FORWARD ACTIONS
Encouraging respect and diversity in your organization

1. Gain awareness of and accept your own cultural programming, which impacts your thinking and behaviors, and consider this programming when engaging with others.

2. Develop flexibility with people who are culturally different, get to know their world views, and understand how their views influence them in the workplace.

3. Take a stand against stereotyping. As I learned in my multicultural training, if you are not taking a stand, you are part of the problem. Have the courage to speak out against mean comments, stereotypes, bias, and demeaning or hurtful statements. They have no place

in your organization because these are the attitudes and behaviors that prevent inclusion and teamwork.

4. Get to know the landscape of your organization. What is your cultural makeup? Do you have a roadmap for its navigation? Learn more about the culture that exists within your organization. For example, read *Coaching Across Cultures* by Phillip Rosinski, which groups cultural orientations into categories that are of importance to leaders. If you really want to unleash the fullest potential in your people, as well as within your organization, it's key to understand the cultural differences of your employees. Besides the obvious, these differences can relate to a sense of power and responsibility, time management approaches, definition of identity and purpose, boundary specifications, modes of thinking, or communication patterns.

5. Make inclusion part of your organizational plan. What are you currently doing to encourage respect for others' ideas? Are you inviting ideas from everyone? What professional development might you or your teams need in order to understand diversity?

6. Encourage talent diversity in your organization. Most of the time, when people think of respect and diversity, there is a significant emphasis on race, sex, and skin color. Few people consider talent diversity in an organization. Urge people to respect one another's diverse talents. Start by giving recognition to the people who perform tasks that would otherwise

go unnoticed. If possible, have some of your more influential team members spend time observing other departments or working alongside people who perform tasks different from theirs. After all, nothing cultivates mutual respect and understanding like walking in another person's shoes. You'll find that the more you encourage people to respect diversity of talent, the more encouraged they'll be to respect diversity of all kinds.

7. Continue to look for, recognize, and value diversity. It makes your journey far more scenic, and it enriches your experience and the experience of others.

To put your results into overdrive, visit our "Enjoy and Respect Diversity" Accelerators at

www.TheRenegadeLeader.com

Chapter 11

Put it All Together:
Living the I.N.F.L.U.E.N.C.E. Framework

"The key to successful leadership today is
influence, not authority." –Kenneth Blanchard

After the merger was finalized, the first item on Jim's agenda
was to bring the entire team together. He flew in the Rumbletree
staff and began with a dinner, reserving a restaurant for their
private evening. He watched as team members engaged with
one another. There was a sense of excitement in the air.

He was warmed with pride seeing his entire team in one
place. It had taken hard work to get there, and he knew the real
work was just beginning. He would let them have that night to
get to know one another, to build their high performing team.

"Who knows what they might be able to create together?" he thought. "It's exciting to contemplate."

Early the next morning, Jim watched as everyone filled the meeting room. He noticed where each person sat and was pleased to see that his team members were dispersed, already welcoming their counterparts. Between the dancing and laughter the night before, he was sure that camaraderie and friendships had already begun.

The coffee was hot, the water pitchers were filled, and much work was to be done in the room. Wanting to stay focused, Jim hired a facilitator for the meeting. In their new tradition, the guiding agreements for their meeting were discussed, and the facilitator began. Jim knew it would be far more valuable for him to be a peer than a leader in the room. He had asked all of his management team to do the same, acting as equals to any team member.

The job of the facilitator was to ask the powerful questions, define the actions needed, and weave the fabric of the vibrant shared vision they would all own and enjoy—one that would set them apart from other companies and their competition, as well as make their company a great place to work. The facilitator would be the container that held the information, holding onto all the pieces so that the participants could pick what they needed and discard the rest.

The clatter of voices filled the room. Jim knew the conversation would never end. It had become part of their culture to question, give feedback, plan, evaluate, be creative, and bring problem-solving and innovative energy into the room. He sat back in admiration and pride.

He could feel the change in the atmosphere, just as the Framework had promised. He had an internal glow, knowing that his hard work had been worth it. He always knew the merger would work, and using the I.N.F.L.U.E.N.C.E. Framework as a roadmap helped him to put it all together with the help of his capable team.

Jim had always been respected for his title, but now he was respected for the leader he had become.

The Questions That Pull It Together

So, what are some of the questions the facilitator asked Jim's team? These key powerful questions create a culture of I.N.F.L.U.E.N.C.E. Ask them in your organization, and you will be surprised by the results.

The first group of questions focuses on who you are as an organization:

1. Who are we as an organization?

2. What do we stand for?

3. What makes us successful?

4. What could we be better at?

5. How can we improve?

6. Where are we going?

7. What is our shared vision?

8. What actions need to take place to help us get there?

9. How will we keep track of our progress?

10. Who will be accountable to keep us on track?

11. How can all of us be involved?

12. What barriers might prevent us from reaching this higher vision?

13. What will we plan for to have the right resources to overcome these barriers?

14. How will we know when we have "arrived" at our vision?

15. How will we celebrate as a company?

16. What is our commitment to our customers?

17. What is our commitment to each other?

18. Why do our customers buy from us?

19. What impact do we want to make in our industry, in the world?

The second set of questions is about values:

20. What are our key values?

21. What do we need to do to live out these values?

22. What do the behaviors to live out these values look like?

23. How will we screen new job candidates for those behaviors?

24. How will we measure these values in our performance review/recognition process?

The last group of questions focuses on your culture:

25. What can we do to get to know each other better?

26. What do our managers expect from our employees?

27. What do our employees expect from our leadership?

28. How do we work to keep the big picture alive?

29. How can we communicate most effectively?

30. How do we want our culture to be identified externally?

31. What is our value in our industry?

32. What do we want to be most known for?

33. What are the media sound bites about our company that everyone should know?

34. How will we "show up" every day?

35. How will we recognize when teams are working toward these common goals?

Epilogue

One Year Later

Jim sat quietly at the round table. It was the end of a long but exciting day. He and his team members had spent it reviewing the past year and planning their vision for the next. Now, at the end of his company gathering, he took the time to spend a few moments in reflection.

Holding a drink in his hand, he thought about the evening he stole away to his study to read the I.N.F.L.U.E.N.C.E. Framework for the first time. He remembered his resistance, but from his perspective a year later, he realized that the company had come much further than he ever could have envisioned that night.

The merger was indeed difficult at times, but it challenged them in the same way a personal trainer or coach might challenge an athlete, stretching them beyond what they believed to be their limits, helping them to see the ripeness of their potential, and keeping them moving even when they thought they were spent. The Framework had delivered what he needed to see his vision to fruition.

He invested in his people, providing the competency training everyone needed to become confident leaders. He also hired an executive coach to be a sounding board for his many ideas. He hardly needed someone to tell him what to do, but it was helpful to have someone with the total success of his organization in mind to give him an objective viewpoint about his actions and decisions.

He also learned how to alter his own communication style in order to have his message heard by his team. For the first time, everyone appeared to be on the same page. Together, they had defined their cultural values and established a common language—a way of thinking and behaving that supported the organization's goals.

He relished the results of the journey. Like an artist looking back at his canvas, he liked what he saw. Their sales numbers had surpassed expectations. His sales team was able to confidently present the merger to clients and prospects. They also crafted the perfect marketing sound bites for potential clients, leaving their competitors far behind in the run for new business.

Merging the technologies and processes of two companies had hardly been without its glitches, but they had managed to integrate, adopting the best practices of each organization. Operational costs were down, sales were up and each person utilized resources more effectively, perhaps because their job had greater importance to them.

His managers had more than stepped up to the plate. They embraced the core concepts of what they learned in leadership and coaching, once they understood how it would make their jobs far easier. They were beginning to use their internal communication portal for engaging conversations and innovative ideas.

But something was as equally valuable as the numbers. Jim had built a company he loved, a company where employees were excited to show up every day. It was a great place to work. Meetings were buzzing with discussion, and employees went out of their way to help one another. While chaotic at times (like all organizations), his staff seemed to have the power to handle whatever came their way.

Jim also had more freedom. At first, it took a bit of getting used to. Fewer crises meant he could spend more time with clients and could be available to his people. He had enjoyed enlightening conversations with team members, learning about their goals, their concerns, and their ideas for the company. "Can I talk to you?" no longer was a sign of something ominous, and he welcomed spending time with them.

Julie loved the fact that he was home more often, getting home in time for dinner, traveling less, and even booking their first ever island vacation. If she only knew he used that "rest time" to take the 30,000-foot view and envision where he wanted to take the company next. He sighed, relaxing back into his seat. This time, everyone at McClarkson would be ready for it.

How ready are you?

What Jim has accomplished with his company is not a pipe dream. In my business, I have seen many Renegade Leaders do the same. And so can you!

As I said in the Introduction, use this book as a roadmap for making the necessary changes in yourself and your organization so that you can ignite people, performance, and profits, and lead with influence.

You can be the kind of leader you have always dreamed of becoming, and you can take your company farther than perhaps you even believed.

As has been proven in my work, all it takes is implementing the I.N.F.L.U.E.N.C.E. Framework in your world. It takes work, but it's well worth the effort—for your employees, your customers, your company, and for you.

How To I.G.N.I.T.E. *Your* Culture of I.N.F.L.U.E.N.C.E.

Learn How to Unlock the True Potential in Your People,

Discover Your True Leadership Capabilities,

and Ignite Your Organization.

There you have it! You've read about the sad status of most organizations today with poor performance, low employee engagement, and the inability to grow and expand due to limited resources. True Renegade Leaders don't accept this as their status quo. Those who take action win the prize of great results, and you can win the same, too!

It will be much more fun once you get started, so before you plant this book on the shelf, decide on the actions you can take to keep up the momentum.

Go to www.TheRenegadeLeader.com to:

- Download the accompanying Renegade Leader workbook plus bonus articles and assessments.

- Complete the Accelerator exercises.

- Sign up for The Renegade Leader newsletter and video training series focusing on key strategies to increase employee engagement, performance, and profitability. Feel free to pass it on to others as well.

- Receive complimentary invitations to executive briefings to bring you the news you need to know now.

- Join the thousands of fans on our Renegade Leader Facebook fan page at http://www.RenegadeLeaderFan.com

- Learn about upcoming leadership events and trainings, and watch for my next book, Renegade Leaders Unleashed!

- Get the schedule for upcoming leadership development resources and training.

- Learn how you can be a part of the business breakthrough or leadership breakthrough mastermind groups.

- Hear about the exclusive, invitation-only Renegade Leader Roundtable, which gives leaders like you an opportunity to rub elbows with other leaders across industries.

- Ready to take action? Schedule a Leadership Breakthrough Strategy Session to break through the top barriers between you and your goals, to receive at least three key strategies for your success, and to learn the best ways to accelerate your results. Contact us to schedule today!

Are You Ready to take it to the Next Level?

It doesn't matter if you are looking to gain results in your organization, department, or even within your own cubicle, we can support your goals. We love to work with Renegade Leaders—leaders who have it in them to succeed, who strive to get results, who are open to new ideas, and who are willing to try what might even feel foreign but promises big returns. We are a bit driven ourselves. In fact, sometimes, we are so committed and excited about your success that we leave a zest of energy behind. We don't work with the faint of heart—leaders who blame others or the economy or who feel so defeated that they swirl the drain (the title of my next book perhaps) unwilling to make necessary changes.

Instead, we invite you to take a real look at your organization, your department, and your leadership style and measure it against what might be possible. It's your time to choose to be a great Renegade Leader. Read on to see the results our clients receive; they can be yours, too!

Join Our Community

Take the first step and join our community. I would love to add your story to the success stories of other leaders my company has worked with. So, share your success! Implement a part of the I.N.F.L.U.E.N.C.E Framework, and we will showcase you in our newsletter as a Renegade Leader! Or simply send your private success story to Debora@TheRenegadeLeader. com, and let us know your progress.

Have a question for the author? Contact us at Info@ TheRenegadeLeader.com and we'll be happy to answer

your question privately or post it on our blog at www.
TheRenegadeLeader.com.

IGNITE Even More Powerful Results

If you are committed to gaining accelerated results in your
organization, leadership excellence, high performing teams, a
culture that vibrates with possibility and innovation, and higher
financial performance, ask us about our proprietary IGNITE
Process which includes:

- A full assessment of your organization, including
  employee engagement and leadership competencies.

- A navigation plan to achieve your unique goals and
  objectives.

- A supported trajectory of the plan, assisting your
  team members until they translate their new skills
  into demonstrated behaviors.

- A review of measurable results.

The IGNITE Process shows you the six shifts needed to
turbo-charge your leadership and gain accelerated results:

Illuminate: Many organizations are so busy that they fail
to take the time to put the spotlight on their current situation.
They lack the courage to shine the light into the darkest corners.
The Renegade Leader Coaching & Consulting Group purposely
shines the light—on your organization, its leadership, teams,
products, and service. You can't move in the right direction

unless you have a complete understanding of your current position. We know people will beat out strategy any day, so we pause to take the pulse of your employees. Are they engaged? Are they ready and aligned for success, or do a few adjustments need to be made to create the high performing teams you need for success? Do your leaders have the adaptive skills of the Renegade Leader's I.N.F.L.U.E.N.C.E. Framework—skills that align with key employee drivers?

Generate: Once you know where your organization stands, you can widen your beam of light, making it as large as it needs to be to generate the biggest vision possible. At this stage in the IGNITE process, you'll ask yourself questions like, "What does my vision look like?" "How will it affect employees, customers, and market position?" and "What will it take in leadership to get there?" We often stand together with leaders and expand the vision, put it up on the big screen, and add surround sound, even stretching it a bit beyond comfortable. We know you can do it. Then, we look at what it's going to take to get there and create the map with measurable mile markers along the way.

Navigate: Jack Canfield, author of the *Chicken Soup for the Soul* book series, once said that all you need to see is as far as your headlights to keep moving toward your destination. At this stage in the process, you'll determine which road you'll travel to get to your destination. I know what you're thinking! There are so many options—assessments, coaching, consulting, training, and leadership development. To further confuse matters, there are workshop-based trainings on neuroscience, emotional intelligence, social intelligence, appreciative inquiry, employee engagement ... you get the picture. I could go on and on! Which of these truly work? The short answer is that all of them work. The long answer is that not all of them will work for your situation. Knowing which tools are right for your people, your organization, and your goals is an art form. During this integral stage of the IGNITE process, you'll learn the importance of choosing a roadmap that will result in positive organizational changes that stick.

Integrate: We customize our trainings based upon what we have learned about your organization, its goals, and the leadership needs of your people. Once you select your roadmap, we will focus on sharing your roadmap with employees at all levels, effectively integrating the solution into your organization.

Translate: In a recent article in *CLO Magazine*, Stephen Parker, vice president of consulting for Blessing White, discussed what he considers to be the some of the common pitfalls and shortcomings of leadership development programs. He notes that at the end of the day, these shortcomings mean that there is very little benefit from leadership development. Parker believes that leadership development programs are ineffective because they:

- Often focus on getting something done quickly instead of taking a full plan approach,

- Are focused on the latest trends and fads and not on how leadership development will address the organization's strategic issues,

- Do not engage participants so that they walk away with a desire to make changes.

What happens when workshop training ends? While many employees leave workshops excited to implement changes, the truth is that what they've learned—and you've invested—is soon lost. As a matter of fact, *Harvard Business Review* states that training is lost within months. Is that worth your investment? We don't think so. That is why we won't provide training all by itself—not when your results are tied to our reputation. We are too committed to your success, as well as our own. Instead, we work with your people to translate what they learned into the day-to-day tasks that are needed for the success of your goals and your vision. We answer the questions, "How do I make this work with my team? With my co-worker? For our objectives?" While we do guarantee that people will feel motivated and inspired at the end of our trainings and coaching, that isn't enough; we're looking for long-term results.

Evaluate: Like any journey, we note the mile markers along the way and assess where we are at any given time. As behavioral and mindset changes occur, you'll be able to see measurable improvements in unity, engagement, performance, and profits. Now, we're picking up speed and cruising down the road, and you're starting to get the results you're looking for!

We invite you to get started and to claim the results that are rightfully yours. Are you ready for a new work experience? A shift in team performance? Unprecedented numbers on your financial statements?

The Results our Clients Receive

We know your dollar investments are just as important to you as they are to us. That is why we focus on bringing in the results you desire—measurable and priceless tangible R.E.S.U.L.T.S. such as:

- Revenues increased and growth of company.

- Engaged employees.

- Strategies for your culture that promote collaboration and accountability.

- Unified values, vision, and behaviors.

- Leadership excellence.

- Transparency of shared vision, values, and goals.

- Sustainability.

Remember, you hold the key. The IGNITE process shows you how to effectively and consistently start your engines, electrify your team, department, or company, and enjoy the benefits of a finely tuned machine. Contact us today to see how you can get started at http://www.TheRenegadeLeader.com. We look forward to being with you on the journey.

About the Author

As the owner of The Renegade Leader, Debora McLaughlin empowers CEOs, managers, and leadership teams worldwide to become influential leaders who ignite organizational performance and positively impact business results. Debora is co-author of *Blueprint for Success, Proven Strategies for Success and Survival* with Stephen M. R. Covey and Ken Blanchard, and *The Roadmap for Career Success* with Lisa Martelli. She was also featured as one of Corporate America's ten most requested speakers and trainers in *Straight Talk for Getting Results*.

An ICF Professional Certified Coach and Board Certified Psychotherapist, Debora uniquely combines 25 years of real world experience in sales, consulting, public relations, coaching, psychology, and neuroscience with certifications in multicultural diversity, executive coaching, and business coaching.

Her clients include Fortune 500 companies, privately owned businesses, non-profits, and individual leaders from companies such as Bankers Trust, Arthur D. Little, Southern New Hampshire Hospital, Boston Scientific, State Street Bank, Homeland Security, Krupp Companies, Thomson and Thomson, Grinnel Corporation, EG&G, Easter Seals, and Great NH Restaurants, to name a few.

Debora uses her intuition, education, and experience to help business leaders understand the emotional dynamics of others and evolve as leaders, activating the leadership style that promotes employee engagement, builds high performance teams, spurs inspiration and innovation, and allows them to take the lead in their respective industries.

A lifelong learner, Debora brings current studies, research, and knowledge to the organizations she works with. Her goal is to create profitable organizations that are great workplaces and to build cultures that vibrate with passion, energy, and direction.

As a Renegade Leader working with Debora, you will gain:

- Freedom from the confines and drama of day-to-day people management;

- A clearer focus on your business and personal visions;

- A fresh ability to inspire your team, handle difficult conversations, and ask for what you need;

- Effective communication with your employees;

- Aligned teams with clear roles and functions and greater accountability;

- A culture of trust and engagement, leading the entire organization to focus on improvements, solutions, and success; and

- More time for yourself, your loved ones, and your life.

Debora's next book, *Renegade Leaders Unleashed!* will be available in 2013.

She lives in New Hampshire with her husband, two sons, and two golden retrievers.

WORKING WITH DEBORA

Are you ready to IGNITE People, Performance & Profits and take your leadership to the next level?

EXPAND YOUR LEADERSHIP WITH THIS VIDEO SERIES BY DEBORA MCLAUGHLIN

Now that you've learned the **I.N.F.L.U.E.N.C.E** Framework it's time to go deeper. In this step-by-step tutorial, Debora McLaughlin will guide you through the top actions you can take to get the results you desire, higher performing teams, effective communication, increased performance and profitability and to gain the freedom you deserve as a visionary leader. With The Renegade Leader Video Training, you'll learn everything you need to know to eliminate the barriers on your roadway to success.

www.DeboraMcLaughlin.com/TheRenegadeVideoTraining

ARE YOU READY TO ACCELERATE YOUR RESULTS?

Yes! Let's Get Started! I am ready to Unlock the true potential in my people, Discover My True Leadership Capabilities and Ignite the Greatest Possibility within my organization.
Apply for to have a conversation with Debora McLaughlin:
Call 800-891-6875 or Apply at:
www.TheRenegadeLeader.com/Contact

 THE RENEGADE LEADER™

RESOURCES

Receive **The Renegade Leader book** resources at www.TheRenegadeLeader.com/book

To visit the latest **Renegade Leader** updates and resources visit: www.TheRenegadeLeader.com

Join the **Renegade Leader newsletter:**

- Receive a laser leadership briefing on how to navigate current leadership challenges.

- See who's "Been Spotted!" as a Renegade Leader and why, it could even be YOU!

- Gain access to resources to continue to support and ignite your inner renegade.

- Gain special follower only invitations to our executive briefing telesummits.

Join the FaceBook community:
www.facebook.com/deboramclaughlinfan

- Receive blog posts to keep you in "the know."

- Join the discussion with thousands of other fans.

- We'd love to hear from you!

Debora speaks!
Wish to have Debora McLaughlin speak at your organization, event or association? Contact us at www.DeboraMcLaughlinSpeaks.com to learn more.

THE RENEGADE LEADER™

Acknowledgments

I must first and foremost thank the Renegade Leaders who have invited me to join them on their journey. It's always an exciting ride, and at times, we navigated hairpin turns together: Thank you for being open to new ideas and, in typical renegade style, moving forward even if you were unsure whether the ideas would help you succeed. It was my pleasure to stand back and witness the success of your organizations, to feel the palpable change in the air. I know you felt it too, because I saw you celebrate it, not only the financial successes, but the successes of the new organizations you created that burst with energy and possibilities. Employee outing days, industry awards, and other types of recognition are indicators of your unified efforts. It has been my privilege to work with you and your teams, and it is because of you that I leap out of bed every morning, ready for another adventure.

Next, my greatest intellectual debt is to those who have done the hard work that allows me to serve my clients as a human browser. I absorb every leadership, organization, and psychology book, research article, case study, and assessment you provide. Special thanks to David Rock, a founding member of the Neuroleadership Institute, who is furthering knowledge about neuroscience and its effect on leadership.

I also wish to thank the coaching community, which has been most supportive in providing the masterful skills needed to make it all work. Out of more than 40,000 coaches, I am one of the 1,400 certified by the International Coaching Federation, which is an honor. I thank you for having the highest standards and providing a skill set that allows me to quickly get my clients around barriers and hold them accountable to the highest vision of success.

Special thanks to my worldwide coaching family, especially my Mastermind group, who encouraged me to own my own renegade platform.

Thanks to the special mentors who have served me along the way: To John Assaraf, a lunch time experience with you let me see greater possibilities in myself and to ask my clients to think even bigger. To Tim Kelley, a True Purpose expert, and to Jeffrey Van Dyke, who helped me to understand my purpose was to serve as the consigliore to Renegade Leaders. I've never been happier!

Thank you to Robert Allen for opening your home to me to share enlightened business guidance and that multimillionaire mindset that helps me to see my business, as well as that of my clients, in its fullest potential. To Susan Harrow, Alison Luterman, and Brenda Scarborough, who connected the dots. To Lisa Sasevich and Melissa Evans, who inspired me to continue to challenge myself while I assisted others on the journey. To Terri Levine for sharing the foundation of what it means to work *on* instead of *in* the business. This is a gift I now bring to my clients and keep active in my own business. And special thanks to my editor, Melanie Votaw of RidetheWord.com, for her insight, genius, and constant inspiration.

Most of all, thanks to my family, Craig, Kyle, and Alec, for standing back in those times I was in turbo mode, for giving up the kitchen table to my piles of notes and research, and for honoring the ideas on stickies that could not be moved. Thank you especially for giving me the space and time to allow my creativity to flow and to do the work that I love.

Thanks to my mother, who encouraged independence and always told me I could achieve my dreams and pursue my interests even if others disagreed. It might be what prompted me to start the Boy Haters of America club in the fourth grade or to later become part of the Future Business Leaders of America organization in high school and, as an adult, to serve as president of the Business Professional Women's organization or to take on the active role of volunteering for CASA for nearly five years to serve as a powerful voice for children who were less powerful. Either way, she inspired the renegade in me. I admire her courage each day as she moves beyond the physical limits that Parkinson's disease brings her and lives life to its fullest capacity every day in spite of those limits. Thank you to my sister, with whom I shared a fun concert tour after my previous books were published, always putting ourselves in the front row. Giving yourself the gift of the front row in your life allows you see it up close and center stage and to have an experience vastly different than if you were hiding out in the darkness of the back rows. I look forward to this year's front row adventures.

And thank you to my two golden retrievers: Poppy for encouraging me and keeping me going by frequently resting her head in my lap while I typed away, and Miles, a golden mix we rescued from a shelter in Alabama, for always slinking downstairs from his warm bed to loyally join me when writing took me well into the night.

Lastly, thank you, readers, for allowing me to be with you and for being open to considering new possibilities for you, your team, and your organization.

Index

A

accountability   3, 12, 14, 23, 28, 48, 53, 61, 98, 126, 158
agreement   8, 53-4, 124
assessments   151, 155, 167
attributes   1, 4, 19, 49, 66

B

barriers   89, 127, 144, 168
bond, emotional   35
bonuses   29, 101, 110
Boucher   105
brain   32, 63, 82-3
Business Leaders of America organization   169
business performance   4, 15
Business Professional Women's organization   169

C

capacity   33, 35, 37, 87

challenges   5, 22, 32, 37, 88-9, 127
chaos   110
checklist   5
clients   2, 4, 10, 20-1, 45-7, 50, 52, 60, 65, 97, 104, 122, 148-9, 158-9, 167-8
coaching   1, 74, 86, 91, 139, 148, 155, 157, 159
collaboration   4, 13, 17, 23, 27, 62, 89, 119, 121, 123-5, 127-9, 158
commitment   16, 23, 34, 54, 58, 85-6, 110, 114, 126, 128, 144
communication   3, 82, 96-9, 103, 105-6, 116
  transparent   17, 95-7, 99, 101-3, 105-8
communication portal   100-5, 115
company   7-10, 15-16, 18-22, 29-30, 40-2, 45-8, 58-60, 69-71, 90, 92, 101-2, 104-5, 109-17, 146-50, 158-9

branding   105
cost   137
growing   15, 97
innovative   29
merged   48
most   15, 112
national   96
new   98, 123
unified   21, 105
company afloat   8
company canvas   9
company cares   35
company culture   5, 125, 137
company farther   150
company forego   101
company gathering   147
company goals   22
company network   133
company newsletter   116
Company Rate   135
company sign   40
company's clients   23
company's culture   17
company's products   46
competencies   4, 32, 63, 66
competitors   8, 16, 46, 102,
   124, 148
Conference Board on
   Employee Engagement   15
contracts   46, 123

contributions   34-5, 37, 74,
   100
conversations   23, 45, 61, 73,
   75, 99, 142, 148, 160
core values   21, 54, 128
   company's   65
costs   15, 45, 100, 103-4
courage   73, 122, 138, 154,
   169
crises   84-5, 89, 149
culture   4, 16-18, 20, 22, 31,
   35, 89, 91, 99, 126, 134-7,
   139, 142-3, 145, 151
culture of collaboration   124-
   5
Culture of Collaboration
   119, 121, 123, 125, 127, 129

D

delegate   51-2, 63, 71
development, organizational
   17
Digital Equipment
   Corporation (DEC)   16
direction   2-3, 21, 23, 29, 33,
   64, 88, 91, 96, 102, 160
distrust   43-4, 49-50, 54
diversity 73, 131, 134-5, 137-9

drivers
  key employee engagement
  4
  top employee engagement
  28, 51

E

e-commerce organization,
  largest 99
effective leadership 89, 124
emotions 32-3, 78
employee benefits 104
employee engagement 4, 14-
  15, 18, 20, 22-3, 36, 63, 86,
  90-1, 100, 114, 151, 154-5,
  159
employee engagement
  statistics 28
employee engagement
  strategy 31
employee feedback 105
employee loyalty 100
employee turnover 49
employees 4-5, 13-15, 17-20,
  28-9, 32-7, 49-53, 64, 73-8,
  86-7, 89-91, 99-107, 109-13,
  125-6, 132-5, 155-7
energy 32, 34, 37, 57, 124,
  153, 160, 167

engagement 3, 16, 20, 157,
  160
environment 35-6, 86, 125
Executive Briefing
  Symposiums and
  Renegade Leader
  Roundtable Mastermind
  92
Extraordinary Leaders 32

F

facilitator 76, 142-3
feedback 52-3, 59, 73, 126,
  142
focus 16, 29, 34-6, 40, 50,
  64, 75, 121, 127, 156, 158,
  160
focus groups 64-5, 103, 127-
  8
  small 61
foundation 17, 47-8, 168
  company's trust 48
Framework 4-5, 19-20, 24,
  26-7, 29-31, 33, 41, 47, 83-
  4, 95-6, 124-5, 131-3, 135,
  143, 147
frustration 64, 72, 76-7, 136
functions 16, 52, 135-6, 160

G

gender   131, 134, 136, 138
generations, younger   13, 133
gifts   87, 117, 138, 168-9
glitches   45, 47, 110, 148
goals   4, 22, 30, 33, 53, 62,
  73, 92, 96, 100, 103, 105,
  107, 152-3, 156-8
group   72, 103, 113, 123-4,
  135-6, 139, 145
growth   2, 5, 9, 16, 22, 27, 29,
  36, 104, 158

H

habits   31, 33, 59, 69, 83
happiness   20, 65
high performing
  organizations, creating   29

I

IGNITE Process   154-6, 158
inconsistency   49
individuals   2, 18, 28, 30, 42,
  127, 134
industries   2, 9, 21-2, 47, 88,
  98, 136, 144-5, 152
inspiration   29, 31, 33-6, 88-9

Inspire Leadership   25, 27,
  29, 31, 33, 35, 37
integrity   52-3, 126
interpersonal conflicts   3, 12,
  23
investment   33, 42, 72, 76,
  113, 115, 157

J

journey   62, 102, 127-8, 140,
  148, 157-8, 167-8

K

key leadership strategies   23

L

language, body   73-4
leaders   1-5, 12-13, 16-19, 23,
  31-4, 49-52, 62-4, 66, 81-2,
  89, 91-2, 124, 136, 142-3,
  152-3
  average   34
  confident   147
  exemplary Renegade   20
  fair   52-3
  good   33
  impassioned   62
  individual   159

influential 27
inspirational 33
inspired 29, 34, 38
inspiring 31, 78
most 3, 26
most Renegade 29, 51
new 91
recognized 21
respected thought 88
showcase Renegade 116
thought 88
top 32
what not to do 82
leaders rush 2
leadership 3, 7, 9-11, 13, 15,
 17-24, 27, 31-3, 39, 57-9, 61-
 7, 89, 100, 154-6, 167
 ineffective 3
 inspired 33, 57, 89
leadership competencies 154
leadership development 90-1,
 152, 155-6
leadership development
 programs 156
leadership excellence 22,
 154, 158
leadership methods 14
leadership mindset, new 31
leadership skills 86
leadership strategies 92

leadership style 13, 17, 21,
 27, 153, 159
leadership teams 104, 136,
 159
leadership training 3, 22
lenders 47, 50, 87-8, 127
listening 37, 53, 72
Long Lived Company Study
 16

M

management 19, 22, 50, 97-
 8, 105, 113-14, 123, 160
management teams 7, 22, 41,
 49, 58, 86-7, 98-9, 104, 116,
 133, 142
 extended 10
managers 7, 12, 33, 41, 46-
 8, 52, 66, 77, 91, 105, 107,
 115-16, 132-3, 145, 148
 company's 103
meetings 7, 10, 23, 36-7, 54,
 59-62, 72, 74, 76, 82, 99,
 102-3, 119-20, 124-6, 142
merged company's employees
 133
merger 10, 12, 29-32, 41, 43-
 4, 49, 58-61, 70-1, 75, 86,
 96-8, 104, 119-20, 123-4,
 147-8

MGM Grand   20, 109, 112

mile markers   109, 112, 128, 157

Millennium generation   133

model   12, 17, 22, 37, 99, 116, 134, 137

money   16, 76, 96, 113

movement   35, 127-8

N

navigate   100, 155

Neuroleadership Institute   167

neuroscience   32, 82, 92, 124, 155, 159, 167

neuroshifts   82-3

O

organization   1-5, 14-18, 20-1, 32-5, 47-50, 62-6, 81-3, 86-7, 99-102, 104-5, 127-8, 134-9, 143, 148-9, 153-6

Organizational cultures   4

organizational goals   3, 74

organization's goals   36, 148

P

passion   2-3, 32, 34, 36, 114, 124, 126, 160

performance   4, 14, 19-21, 50, 66, 101, 111-12, 114, 119, 132, 136, 145, 149, 151, 157

organizational   159

power   65, 81, 84, 87, 90, 139, 149

praise   115-16

president   21-2, 109, 114, 156, 169

pride   35, 90, 114, 127, 134, 141-2

profits   4, 20, 28, 31, 149, 157

projects   33, 45, 51, 78, 89, 102-3, 125, 127-8

R

recognition   22, 110-11, 113-17, 139, 167

public   113, 115

Recognize Achievements   109, 111, 113, 115, 117

relationship building   122

relationships   19, 27-8, 135, 137

reliability   52-3

renegade   1, 128, 152, 169

Renegade Leader   1, 4-5, 20, 40-2, 50-2, 58, 78, 86, 88-

90, 92, 98-100, 124, 134-6, 151-3, 159-60
effective 31
great 72, 153
inner 3, 32
Renegade Leader Coaching & Consulting Group 154
Renegade Leaders Unleashed 152, 161
Renegade Leadership 17
RenegadeLeader.com 153-4
resources 3, 26, 28, 52, 91, 103, 127, 152, 165
responsibilities 1, 18-19, 47, 53-4, 58, 61-3, 86-7, 127, 139
rewards 102, 114, 116-17
risks 51, 54, 92
roadblocks 3-4, 11, 136
roadmap 4, 16, 19, 23, 50, 128, 139, 143, 149, 156

S

sales manager 11, 123
sales reps 42, 45, 122
sales training 76
salesperson 46, 76-7
schedule 96, 117, 152
services 8, 10, 23, 35, 46-7, 64-5, 102, 122-3, 126, 154

shared values 17, 92, 105, 127, 134
shortcomings 156
sign 45, 74, 149, 151
skills 18, 28, 33-4, 76, 86, 90-1, 137, 155
unique 34
social networking 13, 88, 98, 101
social networking platform 97
staff 2, 5, 8, 15, 28, 42, 64, 76-7, 100, 102, 110-11, 122, 124, 149
staff meeting 40, 57, 69, 133
staff members 9, 14, 54, 90, 116, 132
stresses 26-7, 89
sustainability, organization's 17

T

tasks 11, 20, 36, 51, 53, 127-8, 139-40, 157
team meetings 23, 25, 43, 64, 82
team members 3-4, 11, 13, 22, 32-3, 40, 60, 62, 72-3, 89, 138, 140-2, 147, 149, 154

teams 11-13, 23, 33, 43-6, 52-4, 57-9, 61-2, 65-6, 74-8, 87-90, 103, 121-6, 132, 141, 157-8
creative 53
executive 21, 96, 99, 105, 107
high performing 3, 141, 154-5
technology 13, 46, 88, 98, 102-4, 122-4, 134, 148
training 76-7, 104, 152, 155-7
transformation 5, 17-18
transformation teams 64-5, 74
transparency 99, 101, 107, 124
True Renegade Leaders 2-3, 32, 73, 151
trust 17, 22, 37, 39, 41, 45-53, 58, 61-3, 70, 111, 132, 138
building 47, 137
culture of 53, 160
nourishing 23, 50, 54
trusting 19, 53, 58
turnover 90-1, 100, 125, 132, 136

U

unleash 81, 83-5, 87, 89-91, 93, 139

V

values 17, 29, 34-7, 44, 54, 64-5, 74, 78, 91, 99, 102, 116-17, 126, 132-3, 144-5
cultural 22, 134, 148
vendors 50, 87-8, 97, 127
video 97, 106
vision 1-4, 19, 21-3, 25, 29, 32, 35-6, 63, 74, 100, 126-8, 144, 147, 155, 157-8
voices 29-31, 58, 60-1, 69-70, 72, 74, 78, 83, 90, 100, 106, 119-20, 142

W

workforce 3-4, 32, 135

Z

Zappos 20, 33, 110

Printed in the United States
By Bookmasters